What Else H

By Ra[

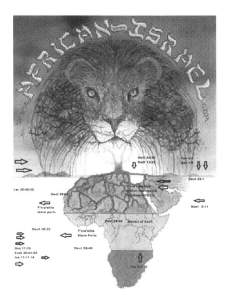

Copyright© 2011-2012 10th African-Israel International Union of Y'sra'elite Qahalim

Revised: 2, Dec 2013
Excerpts can be used from this book without modification for study or reprinting purposes with the set condition that as long as reference is given back to the author and this book.

Rebbe Simon Altaf, BM African-Israel, London WC1N 3XX, England (UK)
Rebbe Lamont Clophus, African-Israel, 8111 Mainland, Suite 104-152, San Antonio, Texas, 78240, USA

Rebbe Simon Altaf for African-Israel International Union of Qahalim or please contact us via e-mail through africanysrael@yahoo.com or phone in the UK +44 (0) 1296 48 27 95 or Rebbe Lamont in the USA: Tel 1-210-827-3907.

Visit our website at: www.african-israel.com

Africa
Contact us for our African contact for all registered Synagogues affiliated to African-Israel International

Gulf: Rabbi John 971 244 63 617

Philippines: Rabbi Robert: 63-908-444-2866

North America Chief Rabbi: Rabbi Kefa Ben Yahudah
Tel: 1-210-827-3907

Other
Failure to get in contact with any of the above people please contact Rabbi Simon Altaf directly in the UK +44 (0) 1296 (48 27 95), leave your message and he will contact you but please do leave a clear contactable telephone number with the international telephone code if at all possible. Or e-mail africanysrael@yahoo.com. Thank you.

Visit our website at: www.african-israel.com

Introduction

This book is as the result of an e-mail conversation with a believer who asked me some questions and one of her questions upon my answer was "What else have they kept from us?" This was the question that led to this book because instead of answering people with small sections of answers I decided the time had come that a book had to be written to answer and address everything as it happened from the start to the end so that many may see that the deception is real and it's a deep cunning deception which starts from your TV screens, in your newspapers followed by wherever you go in your daily life. How would a person know that they are being deceived if they do not know what to look for? Its like a Ten Pound note well if you saw the original then you have something to compare the false note with but what if you were never presented with the original and always had the fake in your pocket then you will likely think the fake is real and this is how it is with Christianity today that is simply mixing paganism with truth. A false Ten pound note or a bad tender which will give you no value when you redeem it as I uncover it in the pages of this book. Who are the real Hebrews? Who is real Ysrael and many others details.

All quotes from the Hidden Truths Hebraic Scrolls Study Scriptures 5th Edition (HTHS) unless otherwise stated.

Table of Contents

Introduction   3

CHAPTER 1 — 5
Christianity as it was in 27 CE   5

CHAPTER 2 — 20
The Cross or The Tree   20

CHAPTER 3 — 40
The Ethnicity of the Messiah   40

CHAPTER 4 — 62
Who is the Contract with Y'sra'el or The Church?   62
Who are the Real Hebrews?   63
The Hebrew marriage removed and replaced by the Greco/Roman model   87

CHAPTER 5 — 113
Kosher or Unkosher   113

CHAPTER 6 — 123
Circumcision for all males   123

CHAPTER 7 — 146
A look at Ezekiel 37 again   146
Questions raised genetic Y'sra'el versus non genetic Y'sra'el   158

CHAPTER 8 — 168
The Sabbath and its abrogation   168
Conclusion   176

ANNUAL FEASTS CALENDAR — 179
Glossary   182

Chapter 1
Christianity as it was in 27 CE

What Christianity in 27 CE? This was the time that a man named Yahushua was an active Pharisee and a Rebbe (Rabbi is a teacher of the Tanak). Please see the glossary at the back for unfamiliar terms. The first lie that is fostered on people is that the believers were called Christians during the first century. In fact the only group that was called Kristianos (a Greek term) were the followers of a pagan deity that was commemorated by Alexander the Great three hundred years before the Messiah Yahushua even step foot on this earth. The believers were never called Christians at any point by themselves but they were confused by others as Christians in Asia Minor which is what we see in the modern bible translations. Let me show you.

Claim: The word Christian is in the Bible so I can call myself a Christian and it is then alleged that Christians believed in Yahushua.

Then the three Scriptural references which are given in the following verses as proof that the word "Christian" exists in the Renewed Contract/Agreement (NT).

> **Act 11:26** (NKJV) And when he had found him, he brought him unto Antioch. And it came to pass, that a whole year they assembled themselves with the church, and taught much people. And the disciples were called Christians first in Antioch.

> **Act 26:28** (NKJV) Then Agrippa said unto Paulos, Almost thou persuadest me to be a Christian.

> **1 Peter 4:16** (NKJV) Yet if *any man suffer* as a Christian, let him not be ashamed; but let him glorify God on this behalf.

Just as one can do anything with statistics and one can twist news and lie about things or make a situation very rosy which is bleak, a bit like the lies fostered on us daily about the fighting in Libya and the daily bombardment one can do anything with the English language but let's just step out of this error and have a closer look at one of these verses. I will be honest with you both politics and religion is about how lies are coloured to present to the people as truth. The Creator gave no religion yet we have thousands of religions today all claiming to be the only truth. The creator described himself as Elohim in the first page and first sentence of the book of Genesis that no religion can claim a right to Him. He only gave that right to one people and that was the people of Ysrael. In order to understand and see the true Ysraelites you need to get the book World War III – The Second Exodus, Y'srael's return journey home and Yahushua the Black Messiah. Ysrael is not what is popularly believed today. Many real Ysraelites will be found right in your own backyard but I doubt you even knew this. The Black Hebrews the ten tribes are in your back yards but you may chase off to the Caucasian Europeans called them Ysrael who are not but Gentiles.

> **Beresheeth** 1:1 Bara Elohim Alef-Tav ha shamayim v'et ha eretz
>
> In the beginning Elohim created the shamayim (heavens) and the land.

Notice the person that described himself as Elohim which can be translated in many different ways such as the following:

The Mighty Ones
The Mighty One
God
The Powers
The Power

There was no room left for debate because being described as the Only Universal Creator it would have been best translated as The Power or The Mighty One. However later Elohim in Page two of Beresheeth (Genesis) gave His name as YHWH this is called the Tetragrammaton or the four letters. Many groups pronounce this name differently. The Term Elohim can be ascribed to judges and angels by the very nature of the word since it means Power so the judges or angels are lesser powers. The word YHWH was also used by some pagan cultures in ancient times and they even associated a consort with YHWH as they tried to harness the power behind the name. This does not mean that unbelievers used the name therefore it no longer belongs to us or that it is faulty in some way.

YHWH gave His people no religion but He gave them a way of life which Noach, Abraham and the rest of our people followed without arguing about its principles. Our faith therefore is not a religion as such but a WAY OF LIFE and you cannot separate our faith from our WAY OF LIVING. Ha Derekh is The Way that even Yahushua spoke about in John 14:6. He never called Himself a Christian or even another label.

When people have a religion they practice that religion in a certain way e.g. Muslims go to the mosque to make their prayers while the majority of Islam comes together on Friday afternoon collectively to do their Jumma (Friday) prayer. The Christians go to their Churches on Sunday while the Jews go to their synagogues on Saturday but what day did the real Y'sraelites go?

As stated we are a Torah law abiding people, we are the real Hebrew people, the Sabbaths (weekly plus the seven annual feasts are called Sabbaths) are set-apart to us, our weekly Sabbath falls on depending on Enoch's calendar this year in 2013 every Saturday sunrise to sunset however that does not necessarily mean that you will find us in some public place of worship on the Sabbath. We may be in a public place of worship but we are equally comfortable and happy to be in our homes with our families doing the necessary ceremonial commencement of the Sabbath because this is our WAY OF LIFE and not some religious fad. As people we may feel like talking and fellowshipping with other fellow believers but we are not into the lonely syndrome. Some of us can be equally happy to be at home and serving Yahushua while others may be outside in an assembly.

YHWH gave us His people, the Hebrews a WAY OF LIFE as stated above and how to live using His set of rules and regulations which we call the Torah given to us completely at Mount Sinai so really we were never at any point given a religion. Originally our Creator told us to build a tent and we had no building but we moved as nomads do from place to place towards the promised land later known by our forefather Yaqub's name of Y'sra'el with a tent in which we would erect our Elohim's set-apart furniture of worship that was set-apart to us. These were the Menorah, the table of showbread and the altar of incense alongside the Ark of the Contract/Agreement/Contract/Agreement where God's glory descended.

> **Exodus 26:1** Moreover you shall make the tabernacle with ten curtains of fine woven linen and blue, purple, and scarlet thread; with artistic designs of cherubim you shall weave them.

We were to extol His name and to serve Him righteously in daily living but our righteousness was not as many nations do today when they drop bombs on others and call it righteousness. As the coalition bombed Libya in the name of liberty but we the Hebrew always measure ourselves against the Torah of Moses which was to be our yardstick. Now tell me how many faiths in the world today do this? Does Christianity measure itself against the Torah of YHWH? If it does not then why does it not? This is because it claims to be the truth and no doubt has many elements of truth in it but it does not practice the full truth of YHWH.

Our faith is a walk and you will notice it is never given a name in the Scriptures, it is not called Christianity, it is not called Judaism and it is not called anything. Even the term "way" from which we derive the term halacha (how to interpret the commandments in the Bible) means just to obey Elohim as agreed within our communities who are Torah obedient.

Now coming back to the pagan deity from where the term Kristianos developed was the deity that certain Greeks worshipped and its followers were called Kristianos, the term comes from the Greek Chrestoi for "good men" and from this the term or title "Christian" came to be formed which was later adopted as a religion much later after the death of the Messiah. The Messiah for which the Hebrew word Mashiakh (Pronounced Mashee-akh) was used was called in the Greek language Chrestus but the only problem was that in Greece and Turkey at the time Chrestoi was used from which Chrestus was developed was a title to a false deity name which was adopted for the term Messiah and this pagan label Chrestus was then put upon the Messiah of Y'sra'el as a title which was acceptable to the Greeks.

Therefore even the term <u>Christ</u> is of suspect pagan origin although today it is not used in the same way. Since the Messiah or the term means anointed in Hebrew and the anointing comes from YHWH Elohim therefore it should be termed as such for instance in Urdu the national language of Pakistan Yahushua is called Masih which is more closer to the Hebrew, in English it would have to be "Yahushua the anointed One" and certainly cannot be called Jesus Christ because the term "Christ" as a title by itself is meaningless. We will look at the term 'Jesus' which is not His real name.

Like all languages English is a developing language in which new words are formed all the time and added to the dictionary. The original old English did not have many letters and in particular it did not have the letter J until five hundred years ago so therefore the term 'Jesus' could not be 'Jesus.' Five hundred years ago it was 'Iesus' because the letter I was substituted for all J's in the bible. John was called Iohn. Joseph was written as Ioseph. The same for Jeremiah. Ieremiah. All these things can be verified if you look at the 1611 King James Version translation and you will see that the name was not beginning with a J for Jesus. Therefore this name is not the Messiah's true name.

Here is a quote from a King James Version Bible the original 1611 edition.

> **Matthew 1:1, 25**
> **CHAP. I. 1 The genealogie of Christ from Abraham to Ioseph. 25 And knewe her not, till shee had brought forth her first borne sonne, and he called his name <u>IESVS</u>.**

Notice the missing letters in the year 1611. This gives evidence of what I am saying. The term Mashiakh in the Hebrew simply meant one who is anointed and this term was frequently applied to the Kings, Judges and prophets of Y'sra'el so there was really no special meaning attached to it just before the first century when a special meaning began to be attached to the term Mashiakh to mean a special deliverer would come to deliver Y'sra'el out of the hands of the Romans which is why Bar Kosiva was called the coming Messiah by Rabbi Akiva in 135 CE when he fought the Romans and he even minted his own coins. Clearly the rabbis debated between themselves who is the Messiah and what are his functions. Some of them thought he is just a human figure who will be the king of Israel and he did not need to demonstrate that he is the Messiah because nothing was really ascribed to this person.

Even Maimonides one of the Hebrew sages said the Messiah would just be a kingly figure and people did not need to look for miracles to know that he is the Messiah.

The Law of first occurrence for the word "Christian"

One would have to prove that the word "Christian" occurred in the Tanak (Hebrew Bible). Yet we find no law of first occurrence in the Tanak whatsoever and it needs to occur at least once to make this a valid choice of word but since it never occurred therefore it can be thrown out and cannot be a word attached to the believers.

Now some people use the term that Jeremiah used in Jeremiah 31:6 to call it Christian but Jeremiah did not say or use the term "Christian" since he was an Y'sra'elite man writing about his people.

> **Jer 31:6 (KJV)** For there shall be a day, *that* the watchmen upon the mount Ephraim shall cry, Arise ye, and let us go up to Zion unto the LORD our God.

> **Jer 31:6 (HTHS)** For there shall be a day, that the watchmen upon the Mount Efrayim shall cry, Arise you, and let us go up to Tsiyon to YHWH our Elohim.

The word for 'watchmen' is Notzarim, which means branches, or followers of the Messiah Yahushua will go up to Jerusalem and begin to realize who they really serve and who or what they are such as not a church but grafted into Israel, the ten tribes. Some people think this is the first occurrence of the term Christian but it is not. It is called the followers of the Messiah Notzarim applies to the first century followers and later followers of Yahushua called the Netzarim. Anybody who obeys the Torah and follows the Messiah Yahushua is technically a Netzar or a branch. One again it has nothing to do with Christians or Christianity. It describes watchmen and those that will go and become watchmen in Y'sra'el the land where the Tabernacle of Melek Dawud (King David) which is fallen will be raised in the coming days very soon.

Let me show you evidence of what king Constantine made people swore who were Christians in his time.

> [1]"I renounce all customs, rites, legalisms, **unleavened breads** & sacrifices of **lambs of the Yahudim**, and all other **feasts of the Yahudim**, sacrifices, **prayers**, aspersions, **purifications**, **sanctifications** and **propitiations** and fasts, and **new moons, and Sabbaths**, and superstitions, and hymns and chants and **observances and Synagogues**, and the **food and drink of the Yahudim**; in one word, **I renounce everything Yahudim**, every law, rite and custom and if afterwards I shall wish **to deny and return to Yahudit superstition**, or shall be found eating with The Yahudim, or feasting with them, or secretly conversing and condemning the Christian religion instead of openly confuting them and condemning their vain faith, then let the trembling of Gehazi cleave to me, as well as the legal punishments to which I acknowledge myself liable. And may I be anathema in the world to come, and may my soul be set down with Satan and the devils. (Underline and bold mine)

There is something interesting in the curse the people of Constantine put themselves in ended up in the curse. The curse that was put on Gehazi made him leprous and turned his colour white, the same way it was the west that took upon this curse and in effect largely followed by white

---

[1] Parks, James The Conflict Of The Church And The Synagogue Atheneum, New York, 1974, pp. 397 - 398.

and white lies. Do you see the irony in the curse? They were the ones who ended up going to take this Constantinian Christianity and spread it out. It had nothing to do with the faith of our forefathers.

Problem - What did Yahushua call us?

You would have to show where did the Messiah ever say that we are called "Christians?" He frankly didn't. The text breaks from every angle, which says that they are Christians or ever called themselves Christians. Sadly most of our Bible translations are riddled with pagan titles because of bias and personal agendas of various people but most of these can be cleared up quickly by going back to the original culture and the language which we know was Hebrew. The Hidden-Truths Hebraic Scrolls is the only bible I know of that clears a lot of confusion and mistranslated or inserted text. There are other bibles that translate the names of Elohim into sacred names hence one can pickup the sacred name bibles to read the true names of the people and Elohim.

I suggest the Hidden-Truths Hebraic Scrolls formerly called the Abrahamic-Faith Study Scriptures as that goes a lot further into revealing the culture of our people and their ethnicity.

The term "Christian" was deliberately inserted to confuse the masses and inject a brand new religion in the scriptures when one did not exist. It was to tie up the followers of Yahushua and call them Christians. This was done by the Roman Catholic clergy.

The Messiah refers to us as "His sheep". This term was mentioned in the Tanak.

> **John 10:14** (NKJV) "I am the good shepherd; and I know **My sheep**, and am known by My own.

The reference in the Torah

> **Numb 27:17** (NKJV) "who may go out before them and go in before them, who may lead them out and bring them in, that the congregation of YHWH may not be **like sheep** which have no shepherd."

The reference in the prophets

> **Ezek 34:6** (NKJV) "**My sheep** wandered through all the mountains, and on every high hill; yes, My flock was scattered over the whole face of the earth, and no one was seeking or searching for them."

The reference in the Psalms

> **Psalm 74:1** (NKJV) O God, why have You cast us off forever? Why does Your anger smoke against the sheep of Your pasture?

Now we piece together the evidence before we arrive at our conclusion.

> **Act 24:5** (NKJV) For we have found this man *a* pestilent *fellow*, and a mover of sedition among all the Jews throughout the world, and a **ringleader of the sect of the Nazarenes**:

Here we can see that Paulos is accused of being a ringleader of the sect of Netzarim not to be confused with the church of the Nazarenes which is a gentile church who are just lawless Christians. How can it be that two chapters later in the book of Acts someone inserts the term "**Christian**" which is a word foreign to the disciples of Yahushua? This is how the text of the New Testament is tampered with and Paulos was the man they could use to achieve their agenda.

You may not be aware that when the King James Version bible was being translated that in one particular verse the name was mistaken for the term "Jesus" but was actually Joshua. So what was Joshua's Hebrew name? It was Yahushua, which can also be written as Yehoshua.

Let me show you the proof.

> **Hebrews 4:8** (KJV) For if Jesus had given them rest, then would he not afterward have spoken of another day.

Do you see the mistake? Let me now show you the correction in the New King James Version Bible.

> **Hebrews 4:8** (NKJV) For if <u>Joshua</u> had given them rest, then He would not afterward have spoken of another day.

Notice the switch that now it's corrected to Joshua. Now you can easily go to any Bible and check out Joshua's Hebrew name.

> **Exodus 17:9** (NKJV) And Moses said to Joshua…

> **Exodus 17:9** in Hebrew

ויאמר משה אל־יהושע

V' Yomar Mosheh Al Yahushua.

I hope you can see this clearly even from the mistake that was made in the King James Version translation that the name was indeed Yahushua and not Jesus. The term Jesus is an appellation from the Latin/Greek from ee-sus to ee-sous. Note that the Qur'an a Muslim Holy book that was written in the 7th century used the term ee-sa for the term Yahushua. This is clear proof from the 7th century that in Arabia the name became known as ee-sa which is the derivative of the Latin/Greek.

Now I have given you proof from the 1611 KJV Bible and from the Qur'an in the 7th century.

Now why did the Father in heaven not just give a dream to Mary or Joseph for His name? The reason is that it's all about **The Name under heaven**. That name given was not Jesus or Iesous but **Yahushua**.

Another appellation you may have heard of is Yeshua. This is the short form but actually has its root in Aramaic and not Hebrew. This was first coined in Babylon (Iraq). In Israel it was used later in the first century after 25% of the Yahudim exiles returned. How do we verify this? This is very easy as we look at Ezra the scribe who used it in the book of Ezra.

> **Ezra 8:33** Now on the fourth day was the silver and the gold and the vessels weighed in the house of our Elohim by the hand of Meremoth the son of Uri'yah the kohen (priest); and with him was Eli'ezer the son of Phinehas; and with them was Yozabad the son of Yeshua, and Noad'yah the son of Binnui, Lewites;

Now see the underlined above where it says Jeshua, it's actually Yeshua in Aramaic. These people were in Iraq and coming out from there so the book was written in Aramaic and we can see the Aramaic form of the name is used and what most people do not know that when they use the appellation Yeshua its actually Aramaic a totally separate language from Hebrew but sharing its Semitic root. So next time you hear people use Yehsua you will know that they are using the Aramaic form but don't even realize it while those who use Yahushua will be using the Hebrew form of the name which is the correct form. Some call Him Yahushai or Yahusha even Yahshaya or Yahuwashi.

When you understand this then the titles such as Jesu are irrelevant because there was no J in the Hebrew language neither in the English language five hundred years ago. The astute man or woman can just go and look at the King James Version Bible from 1611 in any good library or even over the internet and the case proves itself that Jesus was <u>never</u> the name prior to 500 years ago. Remember I pointed out the Arabs in Saudi Arabia never used the modern term "Jesus." In the 7th century they were using the term ee-sa which is further proof of the Greek name which has a Hebrew source.

The transliteration of the name Jesus is therefore erroneous. How a name such as Yahushua become Jesus is quite surprising taking these facts into consideration.

Have you ever thought how would anyone on this good earth find the name "Jesus" in the writings of Moses? They would never find it and be guaranteed to fail.

We must understand that it may be OK from a human stand point to call Him Jesus but from a divine perspective it is better to address Him by His actual name. If you did not know this then it's OK and I would never condemn anyone for it but more people need to be educated and not condemned.

A friend Robert Young quotes in his book **Name above ALL Names** page 75/76 as follows:

> As one author put it, "Once the Jews came under Greek influence, we note the tendency to replace or

to translate Jewish names by similar sounding Greek names." (My highlighting)

[From a quotation of E. L. Sukenik Journal of Palestinian Oriental Society 8-1927, pgs, 113-121, given by Gerhard Kittel Theological Dictionary of the New Testament, vol. 3, page 286.] The Universal Jewish Encyclopedia has this entry: "Jason (Greek form of the Aramaic of the name of Joshua)." [Vol. 6, pg. 42, 1948 copyright.]

On page 110 of The New Schaff-Herzog Encyclopedia of Religious Knowledge we read, "JASON: A Greek name borne often by Jews of the Maccabean or later times and by Jewish Christians. On account of its resemblance to the Hebrew-Jewish name Jesus or Joshua, it was often assumed by Jews inclined to Greek culture or living in a Greek environment." (My underlining)

Of course, one has to overlook their saying "Jesus or Joshua". What they obviously mean is the Hebrew name commonly called "Jesus" and "Joshua" in English usage. Their scholarship is too good for them to mean that "Jesus" or "Joshua" are the correct sounds of this one Hebrew name found written in the English both as "Jesus" (when referring to the Messiah) and "Joshua" (when referring to the son of Nun). In dealing with the subject of what "JASON" is, they are not trying to be exact about the pronunciation of the Hebrew, but merely using "Jesus or Joshua" so the public, in their limited knowledge, will understand the main point.

In other words Robert says that the Name was never pronounced Jesus but as Jason which later got transliterated into Jesus with the advent of the J about five centuries ago.

Robert beautifully sums it like this on page 77 of his book **Name above ALL Names**

> So the sum of the matter is this. The Hebrew name of our Savior was a name first developed by Moses through combining the name of our Creator, "Yah", with the name of his servant – the man today

commonly called "Joshua". He changed his servant's name, which meant "Salvation", by calling him "Yah-Salvation". Therefore, the significance is primarily in the sound of this name that Moses "called" him so that when a Hebrew heard that name spoken he would be hearing "Yah is Salvation". The written form of the name in Hebrew (or any other language) is primarily a group of symbols used to portray the sound wherein the real significance exists.

Of course, one has to overlook their saying "Jesus or Joshua". What they obviously mean is the Hebrew name commonly called "Jesus" and "Joshua" in English usage. Their scholarship is too good for them to mean that "Jesus" or "Joshua" are the correct sounds of this one Hebrew name found written in the English both as "Jesus" (when referring to the Messiah) and "Joshua" (when referring to the son of Nun). In dealing with the subject of what "JASON" is, they are not trying to be exact about the pronunciation of the Hebrew, but merely using "Jesus or Joshua" so the public, in their limited knowledge, will understand the main point.

The prophet Moses changed the name of **Hoshea** to Yahushua in the Hebrew and with the combination of Yud from which we get Yahushua.

Please note the African believers who called out to YHWH called him Yeweh. They did not pronounce the W as a U nor the Heh letter. It appears their practice was to say it in a quick sound. We do have evidence from the Hammurabi tablets that the name was written as Yahweh.

http://en.wikipedia.org/wiki/Hammurabi

We have transliteration of the sacred name in the ancient cuneiform script with written vowels of this language. In 1898 A. H. Sayce transliterated three cuneiform tablets dating back to Hammurabi that clearly said "Jahweh is God."[1], Hammurabi was the 6th king in the period 1792-1750 BC

To sum up the believers did not go by the modern name of Christians and in fact Christians were a form of pagans before this developed with the Roman Catholic Church into a religion. The first century we had a few different groups but they ultimately all followed Yahudit and ha derekh (The way) which became known in our modern times as Judaism. This is why Yahushua said in John 14:6

> **John 14:6** Yahushua said to him, I am THE WAY, the truth, and the life...

Ha derekh as I explained earlier was a name used for the faith and to do halakha was how to conduct yourself day to day in keeping the commandments which was simply referred to as Ha derekh. There were four primary groups of people, the Pharisees, The Essenes, the Sadducees and the all important Galileans[2]. However there were two other groups also one which became the Netzarim movement which comprised some of the Galilean families in which a lot of the followers of Yahushua fitted in because He was from the North of Y'sra'el therefore Netzarim a short term for Nazareth while the word itself means 'Branches.' This came from the famous saying from the prophet Jeremiah.

> **Jeremiah 23:5** Behold, the days come, says YHWH, that I will raise to Dawud a right-ruling Branch, and a King shall reign and prosper, and shall execute right-ruling and justice in the earth.

One group was also known as the Ebionites or the poor ones who did not believe in Yahushua as the eternal Messiah but only a physical man-Messiah and they did not like Shaul of Tarsus and despised him. They removed all his writings from their book they compiled together.

This is the reason why some of Yahushua's followers thought of him as the King.

> **Acts 1:6** When they therefore came together, they asked him, saying, Master, will you at this time restore the kingdom to Y'sra'el?

You would only ask Him if He had authority as a King about the restoration of Y'sra'el. Some of them wanted to

---

[2] Antiquities of the Jews Joesphus Flavious book XVIII

make him a physical king to sit upon a throne and later the Roman's mocked him as a king.

>**Matthew 27:29** And when they had plaited a crown of thorns, they put it upon his head, and a reed in his right hand: and they bowed the knee before Him, and mocked Him, saying, Hail, King of the Yahudim.

Chapter 2
The Cross or The Tree

The purpose of this chapter is to understand where the idea of the cross came in from. The cross or X is an ancient pagan symbol of Egypt. You may have often seen pictures or documentaries of Pharaoh's carrying this symbol upon their chest in the sign of the scepter. If the cross has anything to do with the bible it reveals pagan worship of ancient cultures. The Roman Catholics who designed and developed Christianity as we know it today wanted to give a symbol to the Messiah that would fit with their pagan counterparts so they chose the Egyptian cross. They angled this as a T to make it in to the Roman cross.

When their king Constantine a known pagan who brought together the council of Nicea in 325 CE to give pagan Christianity legalization and to rubber stamp the doctrine of the trinity. He remained pagan to the end of his life asking Christians to get up on Sun-day morning and stand in the steps to give reverence to the sun which they called their God. He baptized shortly before he died perhaps thinking now he can wash his sins but he did not obey the law of God neither did he at all like the Hebrews and in fact hated them and their teachings to the end of his life. He claimed he saw a cross in the skies when fighting a battle that caused him to follow after the Messiah but the cross that he saw was not the Roman cross but the Egyptian cross the X which is an Egyptian cross and of pagan derivation.

It is well known in the ancient world that the cross symbol was associated with Tammuz and his worship this is where the Egyptians got it from. Who was Tammuz? Tammuz was the son of the Black Cushite king Nimrod who married his own mother called Semaramis later known as Astarte or Easter as we know it today which Christianity celebrates in honour of the western Jesus in place of the real Israelite feast called Passover. The idea of fertility also came out of the ancient worship in Egypt and Babylon (Iraq).

> **Ezek 8:14** Then he brought me to the door of the gate of YHWH's house which was toward the north; and, behold, there sat women weeping for Tammuz.

[3]The Akkadian vegetation-god, counterpart of the Sumerian Damuzi and the symbol of death and rebirth in nature. He is the son of Ea and husband of Ishtar. Each year he dies in the hot summer (in the month tammus, June/July) and his soul is taken by the Gallu demons to the underworld. Woe and desolation fall upon the earth, and Ishtar leads the world in lamentation. She then descends to the nether world, ruled by Ereshkigal, and after many trials succeeds in bringing him back, as a result of which fertility and joy return to the earth. In Syria he was identified with Adonis.

Biblically we are forbidden to erect crosses or to even kneal before them but you can look around you and you will see many Christians and Catholics keeling before crosses. The Catholics even have their Jesus the western portrait on the cross as a statue. The real Yahushua was not of Caucasian skin colour but of darker skin as are the Africans today. You can read up more about this in my book Yahushua the Black Messiah from Lulu press at www.african-israel.com.

This correlates with the writing of the disciples that state clearly that Yahushua was hung on a tree and no where does the Bible ever use the word "cross" in the original language of Hebrew but the word itself was introduced into the bible in the late 3rd century to obfuscate the truth, in order to please the pagans who had joined Christianity to allow them to have a stake in this new religion that Rome had created. Therefore all the wordings that said tree, stake or beam were changed with the wording of the 'cross'. Note the disciples of Yahushua did not know of their Master hanging on a cross but did write about him dying upon a living tree.

> **Acts 5:30** The Elohim of our ahvot (fathers) raised up Yahushua, whom you seized and killed by hanging on an etz (tree).

Yahushua was hung on a tree and not on a cross beam, a very important detail according to the Torah. Yahushua's

---

[3] http://www.pantheon.org/articles/t/tammuz.html

punishment for being hung on a tree was simply blasphemy and according to the Tanak and Renewed Contract/Agreement (NT) he took our sins upon Him. The punishment for blasphemy in the Torah is to hang on a tree.

> **Deut 21:22** And if a man have committed a sin worthy of death, and he be to be put to death, and You hang him on an etz (tree):

The Torah commanded our people to hand a guilty person who was put to death on the orders of the judges unto a tree. Nowhere did the Israelites ever put people on crosses. The practice was never done and YHWH never required us to do so. When a person was put on a tree to die then he had to face the holy of holies towards the Tabernacle and Temple but he could not just face anywhere. In the case of Yahushua when he died He too died on the Mount of Olives a place marked for the sacrifice of the red heifer and also He faced the holy of holies. The Romans did crucify many people on the wooden beams that came to be known as a cross but when Yahushua was put to death they the Romans had run short of wooden crosses plus the fact that the Yahudim advised how Yahushua should be killed which was in accordance with the Torah law of putting Him on a tree and then to stone Him to death.

In reality the symbol of the cross is of Tammuz a false deity of Iraq and the symbol of steeples which you will find in many churches is the symbol of fertility used in ancient pagan worship.

Most Christians including of course the Pastors, Bishops and Archbishops are extremely ignorant of our real faith and the real Messiah all the while giving the very late developed name 'Jesus' to the Saviour which is not from the first century. In order to see and know the real Messiah I advise you acquire the book "Yahushua, The Black Messiah by Rabbi Simon Altaf" from Lulu press.

If you want to know who our people were I would suggest the book Beyth Yahushua, the Son of Tzadok, The Son of Dawud.

It should be evident even from the pages of Scripture that our people who were dark skinned did not espouse ways of paganism to their faith and did put people on trees when they hung them as required by the law of YHWH dictated by Musa (Moses).

> **Josh 8:29** And the king of Ai he hanged on an etz (tree) until evening: and as soon as the sun was down, Yahoshua commanded that they should take his carcass down from the etz (tree), and cast it at the entering of the gate of the city, and raise thereon a great heap of stones, that remains to this day.

Why are we told this particular story? This is because we are shown a glimpse of how the law in the Torah was to function. No man was ever put on a cross which is a late development. It was used by both the Phoenicians and then the Romans. It would have been forbidden to hand a Yahudi man such as Yahushua on a pagan cross because the Torah does not prescribe it. The Yahudim therefore carefully put Yahushua on a tree. This was carefully done by the Romans to put Him to death. After His death he was put in the tomb of his uncle Yosef of Arimathea who was his adopted father after the death of Yosef the husband of Miriam. Miriam was the sister of Yosef of Arimathea.

We know Yahushua carried His own gallows that is the transverse
beam called the Patibulum. Matthew 27:32 Greek Stavros meaning a pole or a beam certainly no Babylonian cross as He was hung on a tree with two other Torah believing freedom fighters that are commonly referred to as thieves.

> **Mattityahu 27:32** And as they came out, they found a man of Cyrene (North Africa), Shimon by name: him they compelled to bear his execution stake.[4]

The Stoning of Yahushua

---

[4] The traverse beam is known as a patibulum which would usually be put on the back of the person who is to be crucified. Some criminals were nailed to the patibulum and carried across to be put up. Other alleged criminals were allowed to carry the beam on their back. We can see that Yahushua was in the category allowed to carry the beam.

How do we counter the horses in our lives that are obstacles and obstructions built up by false theologies and the biggest deceptive cult in this world Roman Catholicism and her daughters it went out to be the biggest but YHWH broke it in half and then halved it again. YHWH allowed Islam to be raised up against it.

We usually accept traditions because that is what we were taught to do but we need to look and question a lot of the things to make sure that what we have received is the word of truth and not simply man made traditions with no truth attached to them!

For example one such false tradition is that the Messiah was crucified at the Gordon's tomb (called Calvary). Millions of Christians flock to the place and sing this hymn of Calvary but did you know that this is not the site of the burial of Yahushua? So we know that just because millions of people sing this it does not make it true.

The cross is a pagan Babylonian symbol but the Messiah was hung on a tree as per the law of Torah but Christians are blatantly ignorant of the facts on the ground. Acts 5:30 and First Peter 2:24

A billion and a half people believe in Islam in going to Hajj to remove their sins but the majority of these people going there do not make Mecca a holy place. The most holy place for YHWH is Jerusalem and not Mecca. The chosen nation was and still is Israel and not the Church.

The Church has the arrogance to claim that they have superseded our people and now are the chosen under their erroneous teachings and that they do not have to obey the Torah of Moses.

The Messiah and His beatings…

Usually people do not die from lashes unless they have a very weak disposition. One puzzling thing was that the Messiah died very quickly while on the tree.

How did the Messiah die so soon?

> **Second Corinthians 11:24** Of the Yahudim (Hebrew people) five times I received forty lashes minus one.5

We usually accept traditions because that is what we were taught to do but we need to look and question things to make sure that what we have received is accurate!

Over a billion people believe in going to the Vatican as a holy site to ask forgiveness of sins and some of these even go to Lourdes in France! Yet they too are wrong.

The most holy place established by YHWH is Jerusalem and not Mecca in Saudi Arabia, nor the Vatican in Rome or Lourdes in France for that matter!

Another traditional error says YHWH has replaced Israel and now the church is Israel.

Another conveniently ignored scripture is Amos 3:2 which says YHWH has only a relationship with Ysrael. Yet scripture says: in **Amos 3:2** 'You **[Ysrael]** only have I known of all the families of the earth;

The 'You' is Ysrael.

Another tradition says his name was 'Jesus'. While we have identified this is not His true name. The letter J was invented just after the release of the King James Version bible in 1611 nearly over five hundred years ago then how could he be called Jesus? Yahushua is His correct name:

> **Acts 5:30** The Elohim of our fathers raised up Yahushua whom you murdered by <u>hanging on a tree</u>

Traditions are good if they align with scripture and if not then they need to be discarded.

1 Peter 2:24 is the second witness to the truth of the Tree

---

[5] Paulos was lashed five times, 39 lashes each time according to the custom and law.

The cross is a pagan Babylonian symbol; it's the symbol of Tammuz a false deity out of Babylon. There was no mention of the term 'cross' in any translation prior to the 4th century CE as the words were put in their to align people with the false religion of Catholicism.

Let's examine another truth that few people know about and it is NEVER even discussed in the thousands of established churches. A truth that should be discussed is being simply ignored!

The Messiah's Death!

The traditional account says, he was put on trial, accused and then scourged by the Romans and subsequently put on an alleged cross beam where He died after six hours.

I would like to tell you that this is very simplistic and needs to be examined further.

Messiah and His beatings

One puzzling thing was that the Messiah died very quickly while on the Tree and not in six hours. In fact he was not even six hours on the tree.

Did you know that the Messiah died in less than 3.5 hours on the Tree and not even six hours?

How did the Messiah die so soon?

> **Mark 15:44** And Pelatoos marvelled if he were already dead: and calling to him the centurion, he asked him whether he had been dead a while.

Paulos survived five beatings while we are led to believe that Yahushua would not even survive one beating and last only three and a half hours on the tree.

Why was Pilate so surprised? This is because victims who were hung on a stake could at times stay alive for a few days. There was one case where a man survived the stake for nine days before dying.

The Messiah's beating

> **Luke 23:-21-22** But they cried, saying, impale him, impale him. 22 And he said to them the third time, Why, what evil has he done? I have found no cause of death in him: I will therefore chastise him, and let him go.

The scourging that he commanded for Yahushua was not the customary one which would happen at the execution site.

Pilate was anxious to set the Messiah free so Pilate said he will have Yahushua chastised. The word for Chastise is the Hebrew word Moosawr which is used for when you would chastise a child. You do not chastise a child to kill him.

The Greek word that was used for <u>chastise</u> is "paideuo" and it means "to train up a child", i.e. educate, DISCIPLINE by (light punishment), instruct, learn and to teach.

The word 'paideuo' does not denote violent beatings as associated with a traditional crucifixion.

For Mel Gibson fans his movie is inaccurate on the details. Now we know why Pilate was surprised.

> **Isaiah 53:5** But he was wounded for our transgressions, he was bruised for our iniquities:

> the chastisement of our shalom (peace) was upon him; and with his stripes we are healed.

The Hebrew word for chastised in Isaiah 53:5 is Moosawr described earlier, this represents all the words associated with training up a child like "rebuke", punishment, correction, discipline and instruction.

The Hebrew word paio in Proverbs 22:6.means to hit by a single blow.

Secondly, the blows were not to extract a confession but only to make a big show since Pilate wanted to release Him because his wife had seen some dreams (Matt 27:19) to know Yahushua was a right-ruling man.

The Messiah bled to death

So did Yahushua die so soon? The death was not asphyxia as traditionally assigned. This is by uneducated minds that do not see the full council of YHWH and come up with all sorts of reasons.

If His death was by asphyxia then surely the Messiah should have outlived the alleged thieves but He didn't. The reason is that He was stoned to death which caused Him to die quickly as He bled profusely.

A scholar by the name of Chaim Cohn did some work on this to find out how did Yahushua really die, he wrote a book called "The Trial and Death of Yeshua" He also said that since Pilate wanted to set Him free he would not have Him scourged violently.

> Chaim Cohn said the following
>
> ...if the Roman governor had, indeed, before sentencing Yeshua ordered him to be scourged, as is reported in John and hinted at in Mark and Matthew, he was probably scourged, but NOT TORTURED AS SEVERELY AS IN THE NORMAL ROMAN PRACTICE respecting persons accused of "laesa maiestas," ...but...may have been given several blows or strokes, not with the view to extracting further confessions of guilt from him, but

SOLELY with a view to compelling or inducing him to express regret and repentance and to promise that he would no longer air royal pretensions. -- KTAV Publishing House, New York. 1977. Pages 206-7.

The punishment associated with a regular crucifixion was normally administered at the place of the stake. We know that Yahushua did not receive punishment at the place of the Tree where He was hung Luke (23:20-23). Normally for a criminal he would be undressed and then his hands tied to a prong called a furca after which then he would have to drag this prong to the site of death. When he would arrive there, he would be scourged while being bound. We know that once again Yahushua did not go through this pattern.

We also know from Roman records that a milder form of punishment was enacted sometimes. In this case the criminal would have to drag the gallows to the site of death. We know that Yahushua did drag a patibulum (cross beam) to his hanging site mentioned in Matthew 27:32.

In Greek the word Stavros means a straight beam and not a cross.

The transverse beam (patibulum) was loaded on the back of the one to be impaled, and sometimes he was already bound or nailed to the patibulum when starting out on his final journey. Other times, the malefactor was allowed to carry the patibulum FREELY on his back, and would be bound or NAILED to it when he ARRIVED at his destination. (Clearly this happened with Yahushua)

The Passover Seder is all about the shed blood of the Lamb prefigured as the Messiah. YHWH instructed to take blood of the lamb and apply it to the doorposts of your front door. One needs to ask "the blood that was lost while he was being scourged by the Romans, could it qualify for the atonement that we need?

The Answer! Any blood that was poured while the Roman's scourged him would not qualify. Do you know or understand why?

> **Leviticus 24:14** Bring forth him that has cursed outside the camp; and let all that heard him lay their hands upon his head, and let all the congregation stone him.
>
> **Leviticus 24:16** And he that blasphemes the name of YHWH, he shall surely be put to death, and all the congregation shall certainly stone him: as well the foreigner, as he that is born in the land, when he blasphemes the name of YHWH, shall be put to death.

Remember YHWH hates sin and cannot allow sin in the camp so sin must be expiated outside the camp and any expiation of sin **inside** the camp would not qualify. Therefore if Yahushua died inside the camp then His blood sacrifice would not qualify. Yahushua was executed outside the camp while the traditional sites fall inside the camp another Christian error.

How much blood is needed to remove sin?

> **Numbers 19:3-4** And you shall give her unto El'ezar the kohen (priest), that he may bring her forth outside the camp, and one shall slaughter her before his face:4 And Eli'ezar the kohen (priest) shall take of her blood with his finger, and sprinkle of her blood directly before the tabernacle of the congregation seven times:

The sacrifice of the Red Heifer clearly points to this act. During the sacrifice of the Red Heifer which was the drash (Allegoric symbol) for the Messiah was taken from the Temple to the East Gate in Jerusalem across the arched bridge over the Kidron valley to the miphkad altar located on the slopes of the Mount of Olives where He was hung on the Tree.

Here was the place not only where the RED HEIFER was killed and the blood sprinkled seven times before the East Entrance to the Temple but the Messiah was killed here and His blood spilled. This is what was required. The scourging the Messiah received from the Romans (Italians) was inside the gate (the pretoreum) not outside the camp and would disqualify the blood spilled for atonement according to the Red Heifer Sacrifice.

A pretext for the murder

> **Matthew 26:64-65** Yahushua said to him, You have said it yourself, nevertheless I say to you, Hereafter you shall see the Son of Man sitting on the right hand of Power, and coming in the clouds of shamayim (heaven). **65** Then the Kohen Ha Gadol (High Priest) tore his clothes, saying, He has spoken blasphemy; what further need have we of witnesses? Behold, now you have heard his blasphemy.

As soon as He declared that He was akhad (United) with The Father, the Yahudim there were ready to stone Him but He slipped out of their hands as it was not yet time. Time for what exactly? Did you pick that in the text? It was not yet time for the Stoning of the Messiah. The Babylonian Talmud tells us that a Herald went forth proclaiming the coming stoning of the Messiah which means this was an invitation for all Ysrael to be present.

> **John 8:59** Then took they up stones to cast at him: but Yahushua hid himself, and went out of the Beyth HaMikdash (Temple).

The same thing is repeated in the Temple when Yahushua was celebrating Chanukah and they provoked him.

> **John 10:30-31** I and my Abbah are Akhad (a united one). **31** Then the Yahudim (Hebrew people) took up stones again to stone him.

There is something hidden in this text when you have time read the text of Deuteronomy 6:4 AND THE TWO references to YHWH, the two references to YHWH in there one reflects the Father and the other the Son who is YHWH. The two letters are raised one for Shma and the other for Dalet.

שמע ישראל יהוה אלהינו יהוה אחד

Shama Israel YHWH Elohenu (Father), YHWH (Son) Akhad

The Dalet is the mouth of YHWH that speaks. The Ayin in the ancient meaning as the meaning of eyes to see which is juxtaposed. The picture of Ayin is the legs which are to walk. We are not just to hear the voice of YHWH but to walk it also.

The letter Dalet is raised and the picture for a mouth which means loud speech and points us back to the shofarim sounds of when YHWH spoke on Mount Sinai which reveals Yahushua's orders to us in John 8:32 about keeping and obeying the Torah. He gave strict speech in Rev Chapter one to three for us to mend our ways or else face judgment. If you have come to salvation through Him, then you have entered the correct door through the mouth of YHWH. However, many in the world are still hearing false speeches of other religions looking for ways to eternal life because they do not hear the mouth or speech of YHWH.

He tells them the same thing He did before and once again they try to stone Him. When Yahushua asked them for what reason they intended to stone Him and they replied for "blasphemy".

The prescription for Blasphemy was clear (Deut 21:21-22). Stone first and then hang on a tree. So wouldn't a blasphemer be stoned according to Torah then be hung?

Did Yahushua receive this type of punishment?

They even conducted a make shift false trial against the Messiah in a pseudo Sanhedrin with two false witnesses. Matthew 26:59-75

The High Priest puts the Messiah under an oath and then Yahushua declares to them He is Elohim to which the High Priest tears his clothes.

I want to point out several anomalies. The whole affair started with a woman brought for adultery. Many Christians think this is where the Torah was done away with. The woman is both literal and drash (allegory) for Ysrael and the Messiah who is being judged.

1. There was no husband present of the said woman in adultery. Note Ysrael had also rejected her husband. They did not have the person who committed the adultery with her.
2. There were no witnesses present of the said crime.
3. Yahushua threw the case out of court and told her to sin no more. He did not annul the Torah but He upheld it.
4. The Trial of Yahushua lacked proper procedure.
5. It lacked witnesses.
6. It was an entrapment as per John 8:6.
7. The High Priest was in breach of tearing his clothes as it was not permitted for Him to do this according to the Torah (Lev 21:10)
8. There was a lack of judges, the only person making the decision seems to be Caiphas the high priest.
9. The witnesses were bought in exchange for money. According to the Torah such false witnesses themselves would have been stoned to death but this never occurred (Deut 19:15-21).

Here is another fascinating tidbit.

A lot of people believe and even the Bible translators say that a rooster crowed three times and the third time according to Yahushua's prophecy (Kefa) Peter denied Yahushua.

By the way the interpretation that this was a rooster is incorrect. The crying was not by a rooster but it was by a man who would blow the shofar to announce the feast. These were the people who held the watches (Duties on guard).

There were set watches during which this person would sound the shofar and on his third sounding Kefa denied Yahushua.

So brethren Yahushua was stoned to death, this was the law for blasphemy. He was indeed charged with blasphemy.

Let us look at the evidence from Paulos that Yahushua was stoned to death that is why He died so suddenly and it fits with Isaiah 52 and 53.

Paulos tells us he was stoned just like His master but he survived to tell the tale.

> **Acts 14:19** And then came certain Yahudim (Hebrew people) from Antioch and Iconium, who persuaded the people, and, having stoned Paulos (Sha'ul), drew him out of the city, presuming that he was dead.

Paulos was stoned and left for dead but he lived to tell the tale. Yahushua died and three days later came back to tell the tale but the people thought that He was a ghost but He was real.

> **Galatians 6:17** From now on let no man trouble me: for I bear in my body the marks of the Master Yahushua

What marks?

Clearly Paulos was not impaled so the marks he spoke about were the stoning he had received.

This is why Paulos wrote about the curse of the law which is not Torah but **human** law and government that people think they can be saved through. The curse was enacted upon Rabbi Shaul by a mob really.

> **Galutyah (Gal) 3:13** Messiah has redeemed us from the curse of the *human* law, being made a curse for us: for it is written, Cursed is every one that hangs on an etz (tree): (Deuteronomy 21:23)

The Messiah took the curse of sin upon Him and gave His life for us.

> **Galutyah (Gal) 4:15**…For I bear you witness that, if possible, you would have plucked out your own eyes and given them to me.

Did some people love him to give their eyes, we do not know this but Paulos likes to think so.

Paulos (Sha'ul) had extensive damage to his eyes causing him to see with difficulty. This was caused by the stoning he was unable to see properly after this stoning. The target object of stoning is usually head and main body.

> **Galutyah (Gal) 6:11** You see how large a letter I have written to you with my own handwriting.

Evidence from Pontius Pilate for the death of Yahushua the governor of Judea.

He showed surprise that Yahushua was already dead because crucified victims at times had the ability to stay alive for many days as object of scorn.

> **Mark 15:43-45** Yosef of Ramathayim (Arimathea), an honourable counselor, which also waited for the kingdom of Elohim, came, and went in boldly unto Pelatoos, and asked for the body of Yahushua. 44 And **Pelatoos marveled if he were already dead**: and calling unto him the centurion, he asked him whether he had been any while dead. 45 And when he knew it of the centurion, he gave the body to Yosef.

The scourging that he commanded for Yahushua was not the customary one which would happen at the execution site normally.

> **Luke 23:22** And he said to them the third time, Why, what evil has he done? I have found no cause of death in him: I will therefore **chastise** him, and let him go.

The word chastise is the one I explained above for light punishment.

Evidence from Isaiah

> **Isaiah 52:13-15** Behold, my servant shall deal prudently, he shall be exalted and extolled, and be very high. **14** As many were astonished at you; his disfigurement was more than any man, and his form more than the sons of men: **15** So shall he sprinkle many nations; the kings shall shut their mouths at

him: for that which had not been told them shall they see; and that which they had not heard shall they consider.

The word for "sprinkle" is Nazaw which means to "splatter" and splutter. This is talking about blood being sprinkled on the people of Ysrael.

> **Exodus 29:20-21** Then you shall kill the ram, and take some of its blood and put it on the tip of the right ear of Aharon and on the tip of the right ear of his sons, on the thumb of their right hand and on the big toe of their right foot, and sprinkle the blood all around on the altar. **21** And you shall take some of the blood that is on the altar, and some of the anointing oil, and sprinkle it on Aharon and on his garments, on his sons and on the garments of his sons with him; and he and his garments shall be set-apart, and his sons and his sons' garments with him.

I want to point out two things for Master Yahushua. He is not only the Ram of Elohim, this is the drash (allegorical) and there is a hint (remez) of the future for His sons. Note Aharon and His sons were the only ones sprinkled which means that outside of Ysrael there is no redemption for any church.

No person outside of Ysrael living in sin can ever be sprinkled living in sin, the only ones that can have the sprinkling are the sons of Aharon that is the remez of the sons of the Messiah, therefore the sons of Elohim (YHWH).

> **Leviticus 4:6-7** And the Kohen (priest) shall dip his finger in the blood, and sprinkle of the blood seven times before YHWH, before the veil of the sanctuary.**7** And the kohen (priest) shall put some of the blood upon the horns of the altar of sweet incense before YHWH, which is in the tabernacle of the congregation; and shall pour all the blood of the bullock at the bottom of the altar of the burnt offering, which is at the door of the tabernacle of the congregation.

There are two key pieces of evidence here:

He the sacrificial bull or heifer must be in front of the veil hence the holy of holies. The place ladies and gentlemen is the Mount of Olives and not Gordon's Calvary or the Church of the unholy Sepulcher. Those two places are disqualified because they are not *OUTSIDE THE GATE* an important and critical requirement.

Additionally, the blood was to be sprinkled 7 times. Most people think that the Messiah had to bleed to death, there is no need for this, although the punishment He took would have meant He would have bled profusely but all that was required was 7 drops of blood to fulfill the sacrifice, yes 7 drops that is all but because of the stoning the Messiah actually spluttered blood, remember the verse Nazah from Isaiah 52.

Evidence from the Psalms

> **Psalms 22:6** But I am a worm, and no man; a reproach of men, and despised of the people.

Can you tell me what type of worm is He? A scarlet coloured worm

The other Hebrew word for worm or maggot is Rimmaw, this one here is Tolawth which is a scarlet worm representing the colour of blood taking the sin upon Himself.

> **Psalm 38:10-11 10** My heart pants, my strength fails me: as for the **LIGHT OF MY EYES**, it also is gone from me.

The evidence also suggests that He was blinded by the throwing of stones and spurting of his blood had made Him very weak.

Paulos had full experience of this. The Stoning caused the wounding in the face hence the same for Messiah.

> **Mark 12:4** And again he sent to them another servant, and they wounded him in the head, and sent him away shamefully handled.

Let me give you a verse of Isaiah 53

> **Isaiah 53:5** But he was wounded for our transgressions, he was bruised for our iniquities: the chastisement of our shalom (peace) was upon him; and with his stripes we are healed.

That the Messiah was wounded or broken for our sins, our perversions, and for our rebellion to the Torah. He was crushed for our sins, the Chastisement of our peace was upon Him and by his (stripes) (Hebrew word Khabooraw) **Blows that cut in** we are healed. (Immediately it caused a weal or marking on the skin)

As each stone lands it cuts into the flesh and blood starts to spurt out so that is why we have the front of the Messiah's body marred, the stones striking in his face caused Him blindness.

Isaiah 52:14 gives us the clue that points in the same direction.

> **Isaiah 52:14** As many were astonished at you; his disfigurement was more than any man, and his form more than the sons of men:

Yahushua was a good looking man contrary to error in the Church but this punishment turned Him into something else. This is another area we need to examine, the testimony that we have of Yahushua was that a man of amazing countenance and handsome.

They were always looking to stone Him and on more than one occasion.

Evidence from the Talmud

> In the uncensored edition of the Babylonian Talmud (Soncino Edition), in Tractate Sanhedrin 43a, we read, "On the eve of the Passover Yeshu [5] was hanged. For forty days before the execution took place, a herald went forth and cried, 'He is going forth to be stoned because he has practiced sorcery and enticed Israel to apostasy.

From the evidence presented so far it is clear that Yahushua was hung on a tree on the Mount of Olives as a prefigurement for the Red Heifer sacrifice and He was being stoned while He hung which made him die very quickly under four hours. One more thing if these principles had not been followed then He would not have hung according to the laws of the Torah which would render the sacrifice of no effect. YHWH does not set laws then allows them to be broken by Him. This is only in the imagination, He is very strict on the application of the laws.

Chapter 3
The Ethnicity of the Messiah

The ethnicity that is presented in the Churches of the Messiah is someone of a Caucasian skin colour. This Messiah is also then depicted as the one who abrogated the law of God. Any such false depictions and theologies that are present in the church should be left behind very quickly. In my book "Yahushua, The Black Messiah" I present detailed historical analysis and evidence to reveal that Yahushua was a man of black skin colour and not Caucasian. Also he taught the Law of God and taught His followers that it was compulsory while the Anglo Churches teach you that it is no longer binding. This is the lie that Satan is quite happy for you to receive because all the ministers in pulpits world over are acting as his ministers and not of the Creator YHWH.

Let me present to you something new today that will allow you to see why Yahushua was not what is claimed by both the Catholics and Evangelicals alike.

Abraham a man of Black skin colour who had both Hamatic and Shematic relations. Though Abraham had descended from Shem and was of black skin so was Ham. The lie that is perpetuated by modern Judaism is that Ham though white was turned black after his sin. This foolishness is taught and written in the Talmud that he went in the Ark a Caucasian man but came out black. This is a good lie. In fact Noach was a man of African descent and though Noach was the odd one out of being white alongside his other son Japheth but all the family of Noach lived in Africa. He was of Black parents. His skin colour being white was a sign to his parents. Let me explain. Angels had fallen or more accurately thrown out from heaven after their rebellion in fact there were two rebellions in heaven. In the rebellion when the angels fell who were also Black they were turned white as a sign of judgment.

Let me show you the famous depictions in TV that angels are white is also false while rebellious angels are white the non-rebellious are in shades of brown.

In Ezekiel we see the complete description of some of these Cherubs.

> **Ezekiel 1:7** And their feet were straight feet; and the sole of their feet was like the sole of a calf's foot: and they sparkled like the **colour of shining bronze**.

Anyone will tell you that shining Bronze skin colour is brown which is a lighter shade of Black. This is not a white colour angel.

The angels had made relations with women in Canaan/Israel and when they slept with these women children were produced. Now when Noach was born he was meant to be a black baby but he turned out snow white. His father was so afraid that he ran away. The reason for his running away was because he thought his wife had an illicit relation with the angels who had been turned white hence the white child even though his wife was of black skin colour.

> **Enoch 105:10** And now, my father, hear me; for to my son Lamech a child has been born, who resembles not him;[6] and whose nature is not like the nature of man. His colour is whiter than snow; he is redder than the rose; the hair of his head is whiter than white wool;[7] his eyes are like the rays of the sun; and when he opened them he illuminated the whole house.

Lamech was of black skin colour and Noach his son was born an albino in fact complete white not just white skin but even his hair was white yet woolly like African style. Note his hair is like wool which is indicative of like African people's hair style so his colour of white or the colour of his son Japheth being white did not make them Europeans. However it was through Japheth that the European races and other Caucasian races descended.

Here are some pictures of what ancient Hebrews looked like.

---

[6] His father was black.

[7] This was an albino child completely white an enigma not seen before by Black Israelites.

A Y'sra'elite being taken by Rome as a captive.

Y'sra'elties taken as captives in the Assyrian Exile. Notice the locks on their hairs and very beautiful braided beards. NO they do not have fifteen foot beard.

Notice both Miriam and Yahushua are black. This is because they were both born on the African continent and the African continent was always inhabited by dark races this includes the descendants of Shem both including Ysraelites and the descendants of the sons of Ham.

While Rome and the rest of the Church system has sold you the counterfeit goods. This is one of the pictures of the so called Caucasian Yahushua below.

Does this look anything like the original? Even though we are forbidden from making images of Yahushua one can find the images of Yahushua drawn after his birth were in fact of him as a black baby with a black mother. So if Yahushua was black then what about His other earthly family in Israel? They too were people of Black skin colour. You can read more of this in my book Yahushua, the Black Messiah.

Every TV channel meaning Christian ones portray Yahushua as a person called Jesus and the many of them have his picture as if he is a Caucasian man. This deception is very wide spread by the west also into the east. Its surprising that all these people claim to have the Holy Spirit the mother Chokmah but the only problem is whatever spirit they have it's not the mother Chokmah but some weird He spirit. The Holy Spirit is feminine and they have distorted even this teaching. However to date their version of the Holy Spirit has not told them that Yahushua is black. Very surprising isn't it?

Yahushua is indeed the Messiah sent by Elohim but this western Jesus that is taught in churches apparently teaches people to break the law of Elohim and not to keep the things of the law. They have tried to sell this to the whole world that His name was Jesus and that he was a Caucasian with blond hair and blue eyes but this is the false picture of Him. They are only promoting a picture of Borgia Cesare who was a corrupt illegitimate son of the Pope Alexander in the 16th century.

Here are some images of Borgia.

You may say I don't love Borgia but I love Jesus.

Well here is 'Jesus' the Caucasian looking one who was taken from pictures of Borgia. Its one and the same man.

The majority of the pictures that are used for the purported 'Jesus' today are of him. Also in many pictures Yahushua does not look like a man but a woman with straight long hair. However in reality He had locks and wooly hair. This can be seen in the book of Rev 1:14.

Yahushua was a baby of colour and not a Caucasian looking child smiling in his little baby cot as most would like to imagine or even the imaginary manger is a good western embellishment. How about this black baby being put into an animal feeding trough instead of a manger.

Matrilineal descent to kingship a thoroughly African affair

Yahushua was born to his mother and recognized through the mother as the King. Accession to the throne in both Ancient Egypt and the African culture was through the mother. If some of you are still wondering how this can be then you need to take a sneak peak around the world which still carries the African culture in various peoples of the world at different levels of inception.

The Cherokee Red Indians of North America
The Minangkabau people of Sumatra in Indonesia
The Mosuo of China
The Garo of India
The Tuaregs of North and West Africa
The Basques of Spain and France

All the above cultures descended from the African culture whether they believe it or not. The origin is thoroughly African and their practices also the same in terms of how they accede to the throne.

Yahushua likewise could not claim kingship if he was solely coming from the father this unfortunately many do not understand that Yosef though his adopted father had died when Yahushua was young. Any firstborn child through Miriam could be given over to kingship that was agreed by the great Sanhedrin long before Yahushua was born. These were the children of Yahushua III who was the son of Shimon.

Yahushua's name even was patterned after the forefathers as it occurred back in Abraham's day. Yahushua III was the great grandfather of Yahushua who was linked to Miriam's family so when Miriam was married to Yosef her firstborn son would be given the name of the father or grandfather. This pattern follows earlier when we see Abraham's wife Keturah giving her firstborn son the name of Yokshan (Gen 25:2) a variant of Yoktan since she was the daughter of Yoktan the Elder, the son of Eber

(Gen 10:25). This shows us that Yahushua III was actually related to Yosef's family also.

So we have the following diagram:

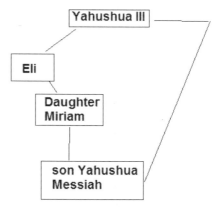

We see the same kinship pattern as I said earlier with Abraham's wife Keturah living in the South however in this case Miriam was in the northern territory the wife of Yosef while Yosef was known to have been married before and we are not told of his earlier family which most believe had died but its likely that his son in the south could not accede to the throne. Read more in Beyth Yahushua the Son of Tzadok, the Son of Dawud the ancient patterns of our Patriarchs the book that busts a lot of myths at www.african-israel.com.

Notice the pattern that Isaac followed when married his second wife at forty. His first wife not mentioned in the Torah who was in the south but he married his northern wife the number two wife called Rebeccah since they needed an heir for the Northern territory and Jacob became that heir while Esaw sold his birthright. So what does this tell us? Isaac had another son from his first wife which is never revealed in the Torah it is what we call the hidden son. Yahushua was also the hidden Son of the Father in heaven revealed to Y'sra'el at a latter time in history from the prophets but many rejected Him in Y'sra'el and even do to this day thinking their brand of religion will save them.

The other problem that most people are not aware of is that there was no person called 'Jesus' in the first century but there was a person called Yahushua and his name was not magically selected out of a hat but commanded by the Father in heaven to be communicated to Miriam as Yahushua (Luke 1:35) by the messenger of Elohim. Just because we read in the English Bible it says 'Jesus' we automatically assume incorrectly that this was His name. In the Greek bible it is Iesous so why was it not Iesous then? In the Qur'an it was Esa. So why not Esa? None of these, but it was Yahushua in the original Hebrew text which was the language used to write the writings the Ketuvim Netzarim that came to be known as the New Testament using a modern word. They did not call the scroll of Mattityahu New Testament by the way!

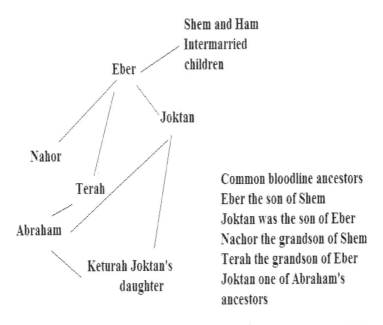

Yahushua was an African through and through and his kingship upon the throne was not some mystical affair as it's made out to be but was a pattern going back to Abraham in which His royal princely line and priestly line were matriarchal. Abraham would have become the High Priest of the temple of idols that his father managed for the ruling King Nimrod had Abraham stayed in South-Eastern Turkey where he was born. The question is who were these idols, figurines in the father's temple? Were they gods as many incorrectly understand or were they ancestors that were worshipped and believed to have powers beyond the grave? Nimrod clearly knew YHWH as the text suggests in Gen 10:9 then why did he go to the idols to ask for help? Nimrod's culture hardly understood by Christendom today so they come to their own erroneous conclusions. Not all Afro/Asians were polytheists in the past but they had belief in one central power and other subsequent lesser powers. We see this in Laban in Gen 24:50 or did you believe that Abraham was going to seek a wife for his son among the polytheists?

Abraham was a prince (Gen 23:6) and was also matrilineally descended through his mother's line who was the daughter of a priest in Karnak to become the High Priest for his father's house but he rejected that lifestyle of reaching to the idols for powers but instead served YHWH from a young age. He was singled out by Elohim to be given the noble birth of a ruling son through his wife Sarah and to have his seed (Yahushua come through Isaac) placed on the throne one day. Sarah from an African tribe today found in the region of Chad (A princess) (Matrilineal) even though Abraham already had eight sons from three wives while Isaac was the 9th Son and probably the youngest of the others. Note the number nine is important in the Bible.

The Bible clearly shows us this matrilineal pattern for kingship while the headship of the house was Patrilineal (Num1:2) but the ascent to the throne or rulership was always matrilineal. This is why in order to be a Yahudi one has to come through the line of the mother (Lev 24:10, Deut 7:1-5, Ezr 2:59-63) while anyone can become a Hebrew Y'sraelite by conversion but in order to be a Levite Priest, High Priest or King in Y'sra'el meant certain biological necessities had to be met. Gentiles were always welcome to join on to our nation and be counted as an heir to the promises given to Abraham our father but a gentile could not become a Priest or a King of Y'sra'el as that was strictly forbidden and still is (Deut 17:15, Num 25:11).

So in essence both Borgia his pictures and the man 'Jesus' that has been portrayed in public are false symbols and love for any of these is misplaced. Our love needs to be placed with the Messiah of Y'sra'el who is Yahushua and who demands Torah obedience from us to be his disciples (John 8:31). Failure to comply means that this wishy washy love that Christian have is of no use. One may well ask how can we keep Torah while in exile and without a Temple and or the Tent of meeting?

The answer is simple, look at the example of the prophets. Look how Jeremiah, Ezekiel and Daniel lived in exile. We are to cease from sacrifices in the absence of the Temple and its priesthood while we continue with the food laws, the seven celebration observances and obeisance in synagogues or homes. Basically anything that required the Temple is suspended until the rebuilding of the Temple and what could be observed outside the Temple can still be done today.

> **John 14:21** He that has my commandments, and <u>guards and does them</u>, it is he that loves me: and he that loves me shall be loved of my Abbah, and I will love him, and will manifest myself to him.

How can you GUARD something that you do not believe in? Christendom is guilty of this sin. Guarding what they think to be only for the Yahudim and doing the things that the Torah forbids. If you have been a Christian returning from Babylon then welcome home. It's not reforming churches but leaving them to reform yourselves and joining on to a congregation that respects the laws of the Most High El.

All the idolatrous pictures of Borgia or this fake 'Jesus' should be removed and binned so that we are not in idolatry. However the signs that our homes need to have is the doorpost Mezuzah, a Menorah and a Shofar. The rest is additional such as Tallits. We wear our head covering for our worship and men keep beards as is normal amongst Y'sraelites. Women must avoid trousers and dress as women and not as men receiving the honour in our homes that they deserve as our wives, sisters and mothers. If you have joined on to Y'sra'el know this that this is a privilege and honour bestowed upon you then you should act accordingly with the utmost regard to Torah to honour the Master YHWH and to keep our prestige of the nation of Y'sra'el. Our Master Yahushua and His Father will come to you and love you if you first show your love through obeying the commandments (Torah).

All Caucasian races have their beginning in the Caucus mountains region which was known as Ashkenaz. Who is Ashkenaz in the bible?

> **Gen 10:3** The sons of Gomer were; Ashkenaz (European), Riphath, and Togarmah (Turkey).

Who was Gomer?

> **Gen 10:2** The sons of Yapheth were Gomer, Magog (Turkey), Madai, Yavan, Tubal, Meshech (Turkey), and Tiras.
>
> **Ezek 38:2** Son of man, set your face against Gog, the land of Magog, the chief prince of Meshech and Tubal, and prophesy against him,

Does that tell us something? Yes Gog is the enemy of Israel. Which Israel? The real deal which is yet hidden from many eyes while most Christians are not even aware of this fraud being purported upon the world where a false Israel is raised to the point of worship.

So how can Israel being Caucasian attack itself if it's Gog. This is because it's describing the people of Turkey who are Caucasian looking but the modern Jews today are also the sons of Japheth just like the Turkic people so they are really brothers to them apart from the two being in different religion but modern Israel used the ancient flag of a Turkic kingdom. The modern Jewry of Ashkenazim origin is also Turkic.

You may be surprised to know that Yahushua was indeed black, a man with woolly hair and bronze skin. He was not blond, white with blue eyes. This is the false photo that was created of him by the Europeans, influenced by the power of the Catholic Church that has been making its rounds in many churches even today. The majority of the ancient Churches still carry Yahushua's photo as a black man then why the charade by Western Christianity?

This is because the Europeans could not see Elohim being black. How could He be black since in the western minds black is inferior. The whole idea of slavery was born out of the notion that blacks are inferior beasts and can be enslaved. This was used to justify slavery while the African people had been cultured for thousands of years just look at the pyramids they built but on the opposite scales the white races were still backward at that time fighting for food. The Greeks revered the blacks and took their wisdom from the black people and then just coloured it as their own. Many of the so called Oracles that the Greek people employed were taken from Egypt and they were black women who called themselves the oracles. You may have heard this term in movies but an oracle is someone who claims to receive or understand revelation; the only problem is they give credit to false gods.

Notice also that the Arabs used blacks to build up their armies the Berbers and Moors invaded Europe to conquer Spain and then left a lasting influence on architecture and science and even in English names. You can look at the evidence by examining the 10th century Spain when berbers ruled it to the 10th century England. Compare the castles, the houses in both Spain and England and see if you can spot the difference. The Muslims ruled Spain for eight hundred years leaving a lasting legacy. The rulers in Muslims the Moors were our own people who were forcefully converted into Islam but they were originally Israelites.

Today the name Moor is actually a family name amongst the English that can be traced to the Moors who were Black. As you will read the Moors were a warrior class of people and in no time demolished all the forces of European Spain. This should give us a glimpse of North African warrior class who were exceptional seasoned fighters. African people have generally known to be natural fighters just look in the boxing world how many boxers are Black and very good boxers.

In Africa there were tribes that had fighters that could kill lions with bare hands combat. That should remind us of another person who had many African ancestors who would kill many with bare hands the man Samson of the Bible. He was indeed black with locks IN HIS hair and only black folks have locks. Caucasian people do not have locks in their hair naturally. Remember Samson's locks became his downfall with Delilah but it does not mean he did not have a calling he did and served his purpose.

It may be shocking to learn this but European Spain was ruled for over 800 years by Blacks, yes black people from North Africa.

One more thing as you can see the Popes specially stood in front of and prayed to the Black Madonna while telling the world to pray to the white Madonna they had carved up to fool the people into idolatry while themselves prayed to the black picture of Miriam who they considered gave them real spirituality.

How could a Caucasian looking Pope pray to the Black Miriam? He would feel shame doing it publicly but also its idolatry so they did it without telling the people.

If Yahushua WHO IN ERROR is called 'Jesus' in the West was white then why does He have his ancient pictures in Ethiopia and other eastern nations as a black baby?

Although there are many powerful men around the world and have been in history but the class of strength exhibited by the Hebrew Israelites was unparalleled by any in history.

> **Gen 30:5-6** And Bilhah conceived, and bore Yaqub a son. **6** Then Rach'el said, Elohim has judged my case, and He has also heard my voice, and given me a son: therefore she called his name Dan.

Bilhah was Rachel's maid who was Laban's daughter given over to Jacob as wife and Bilhah gave birth to Dan. I will prove it here that all the tribe of Dan was Black because Bilhah was a Black woman married to a man with African ancestors that is Jacob and his father in law Laban. Laban in Hebrew means 'white,' which is why his name tells us in Hebrew that he was a 'white' albino. Albinism is a common disease in the African people. This was not often that a black family produced an albino child but he though was from a black family turned out white as often this happens in Africa.

According to the rabbinic traditions and the Targum of Jonathan Gen. R. lxxiv. 14, Bilhah was one of the daughters of Laban. If this is true then we can see the same pattern of kinship in the family line of Laban as we see in Abraham. Laban had at least two wives and two concubines one which was given to him was the daughter Bilhah and the other was Zilpah, they were twins born to his wife Adinah.

The book of Jasher tells us the following: *30:13 And Laban had no sons but only daughters, and <u>his other wives.</u>* This proves my thesis is correct. He did get sons later because of Jacob's spoke benedictions over his house. Beor was the son born to Laban and should ring a bell because he was indeed African and black. One of his sons Bela who is mentioned in the book of Jasher which you can purchase from the www.african-israel.com website with commentary and read the history missing in the book of Genesis. He was from a region in ancient times called Dinhabah which is the modern city in Tanzania called Anabah (Jasher 57:41) and this was ruled by the king of Africa, this man Bela was crowned king over Esaw's people (Jasher 57:42). Well unless you are going to tell me Tanzania is inhabited by white Europeans it is in fact part of Africa and has black people in it too. Also note the original inhabitants of Australia the aborigines are from Tanzania and you can go check their colour to verify what I have said is true and factual and not just conjecture.

We can trace this using kinship analysis to point out where these ladies came from or who was their father or grandfather. Bilhah names her firstborn son Dan and Zilpah names her son Gawd. Many people in modern times confuse this with the term God as a false deity name. There is no ancient deity by the name of God but in ancient times there were towers erected to serve false gods and as such the term is derived from the Hebrew word 'migdol' which means a prominent tower and the Hebrew term God or Gawd is a derivative of this. Let me show you. M'gd-l In Hebrew this would be a Mem, Gimel, Dalet and a lamed. In the most ancient Hebrew language it means, "In the hand of strength."

So one can see Samson was a black judge mighty in strength. The tribes in Ethiopia or the Beta Yisrael identify themselves with the tribe of Dan and they are all black. Contrary to popular belief the Danish are not Danites. This is a popular folklore more than anything else there is no real connection between them and the real Hebrews of Dan.

The term בלהה has the same sound and close association with a word in our language or Urdu from the Aramaic script called Balah which means something that scares or frightens you. This is why the Hebrew of Bilhah does not mean as many attest timid. This is a modern definition.

It in fact means one that unleashes terror. The Hebrew word used for terror is Behelah and has close associations with this term. The other term Balah in Hebrew means 'to wear out' so the combination of these tells me the correct meaning of Bilhah is what I described above. We know this is the meaning because the term Belial is a derivative of this word which means the 'prince of demons' and what do demons generally do? If you saw one they would instill terror in you, you will not be smiling but running for your life. The ancient Hebrew picture of this word is a house, a staff and two men jumping up praising Elohim which indicates this shows a house of strength or one that contains strength.

The tribe of Dan were the tribe of Judges as law makers one's who made sure YHWH's law was followed. When Samson would have walked the streets people would have been extremely scared of this very strong man because he had no match in the land so one can see why names in Hebrew culture have meanings behind them to personal character and traits. Genesis 29:2 tells us that the family of Laban controlled water resources as his daughter was near a well when Jacob first saw her.

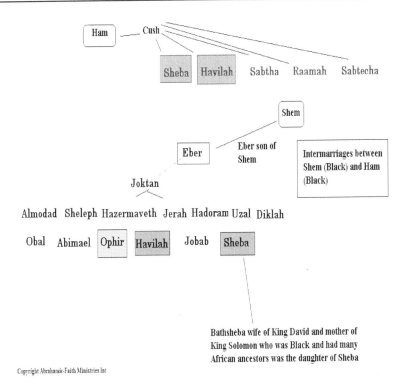

Is Colour and race important?

One question that continues to fester is about colour and race. On one discussion with a black Hebrew the argument went something like this, "Colour does not matter it's of no consequence and Yah did not choose us because we were of black colour." Then the following scripture is quoted to defend the irrelevance of colour.

> **Debarim (Deuteronomy) 7:7-8** YHWH did not set his love upon you, nor choose you, because you were more in number than any people; for you were the fewest of all people: **8** But because YHWH loved you, and because he would keep the oath which he had sworn unto your ahvot (fathers), has YHWH brought you out with a mighty hand, and redeemed you out of the Beyth (house) of slavery, from the hand of Pharaoh King of Mitzrayim (Egypt).

I want to set forth an important point. The Most High El YHWH created only in one colour. This does sound radical and shocking but this is reality.

That is right he only created in one colour and that was <u>BLACK</u> and from that one colour all the other colours came out. When we examine history accurately then we discover that most races had a common black ancestor, like the Chinese, the Japanese moors, the Indians etc, etc. This creation in black colour was not about superiority but what was being revealed. The first man Adam was in the likeness of Adam Kadmon or the prototype of man who is also the Messiah Yahushua. So what colour is Adam Kadmon?

It is a known fact that the human colour black has more melanin or pigmentation. So when you see other colours all you are seeing is less of the pigmentation melanin. If you start removing the pigmentation from skin it starts to change shades to dark brown light brown and white etc.

Let me now show you something in the ancient most Hebrew script. Her name is Chava which appears as follows: Khet, Yud and Heh חוה.

The modern Hebrew picture is meaningless and tells us nothing but let us look at the ancient Hebrew picture to understand it's real meaning.

The ancient Hebrew language was of pictures like the Chinese writing is today. A picture tells the story of the word being described. Ancient Hebrew was a monosyllable language.

The first character Khet reveals to us the whole picture with the meaning of Concealment, of Darkness and of the Bosom. Chava was black this is identified in the khet the first letter of her name. It was not a two or three letter roots as believed. One character defines the word and the rest gives shape to the word in further explanation. So these pictures mean Black or dark living creature of beauty like a bird. Is it ironic that in the British and some other cultures the slang term "bird" came to signify a beautiful woman. The analogy actually goes back to our mother Chava who had the character Wav which signifies the feather in the ancient text and not the description of nail which is a later development

What colour are the angels?

Will an Indian child or an African child see an angel as white? No. An Indian child will likely see an angel in their own colour unless that child has been exposed to western movies. An African child will see an angel in their own colour.

A Caucasian child will see an angel as white so who is correct.

All the children fit the angel into their own category of colour so you cannot fault the children. However now imagine this that the black people who went through the worst kind of slavery will they see a white angel considering the Caucasians enslaved our people? Will he want to submit to the alleged superior colour of white as believed by many when he realizes that they were killed and hung on trees?

Will they see Yahushua as white? Well after much brain washing yes but in reality many will have a hard time to do this.

What does scripture describe angels as?

> **Ezek 1:7** And their feet were straight feet; and the sole of their feet was like the sole of a calf's foot: and they sparkled like the colour of shining bronze.

Ezekiel is describing YHWH's portable thrown the merkabah and it is carried by Black/brown angels. These were not white Caucasian angels.

Further proof that the angles were of black colour.

> **Ezek 1:13** As for the likeness of the living creatures, their appearance was like burning coals of fire, and like the appearance of torches: moving

back and forth among the living creatures; and the fire was bright, and out of the fire went forth lightning.

So ask yourself what colour was Yahushua.

The Point of reference.

- Abraham was black. (He is called the son of Abraham Matt 1:1).
- Jacob was black.
- Moses was black.
- David was black.
- King Solomon was black so he is described as from the line of King Solomon.
- Miriam was black.

But hang on a minute was King Dawud not describe as ruddy?

When you create bad translations then you make people something they are not. This has been fixed in the AFN Study Bible by the way which can be purchased from the AF website www.african-israel.info.

First Samuel 16:12 And he sent, and brought him in. Now he was reddish-black, and of pleasent looks.and handsome to look at. And YHWH said, Arise, anoint him: for this is he.

The Hebrew word is והוא אדמוני ve hu Admony which means he was red/black.

The Hebrew word for white is Laban, so when a person turned leprous he became white.

Lev 13:4 If the bright spot be white in the skin of his flesh, and in sight be not deeper than the skin and the hair there be not turned white (Laban); then the kohen (priest) shall shut up him that has the disease seven days:

Lev 13:4ואם־בהרת לבנה :

V am baharet Labaneh. The root word there in Leviticus 13:4 is Laban, which means to be white.

Why portray Yahushua as white? This was the deception organized by the Catholic Church which then had all of Yahushua's black paintings removed and commissioned white European style paintings to be made in which all too often the African Yahushua looks too much European.

> **Rev 12:9** And the great dragon was cast out, that old serpent, called the Devil, and Shaitan (Satan), which deceives the whole world: he was cast out into the earth, and his heavenly messengers were cast out with him.

Satan actively deceives the whole world. We were punished for sin so as a result even our identity was faded by the nations and they worked hard to eradicate our identity. The reason was our own disobedience to Torah.

Some Europeans have tried to manufacture Egyptians as light skin which is not true. They even deliberately falsified pictures and images.

The real identity of Yahushua will now go forth and no one can stop this. Those that are deceived by a European looking Yahushua will only further deceive themselves but those that want to serve Eloah will receive revelation. Amein.

Chapter 4
Who is the Contract with Y'sra'el or The Church?

One of the deceptive lines that is followed by many Churches is that they have a Contract/Agreement/Contract with the Al-Mighty Creator to teach eternal truths. They have created new laws organized by the Church system which was originally the Roman Catholic Church which later broke up into the Protestant Church followed by many splinter cult groups with around 38,000 denominations and then these push these out various teachings based on their own particular agenda to the people as some kinds of holy decree. Is it true that the Churches have a Contract from YHWH to do this? Let us have a look.

In the ancient system the word Church was solely applied to the pagan temple, even when William Tyndale before being burnt on the stake by Rome translated the one instance of the word church for a pagan temple.

> **Acts 19:37** For you have brought here these men, which are neither robbers of temples (**Churches**), nor yet blasphemers of your female mighty one.

We have followed in line with William Tyndale who translated this word into 'churches' in his Tyndale translation of the bible as every other word in the Renewed Contract (NT) for church was translated as 'congregation' by him. So the word church was seen by one of the renowned English Scholars with a pagan temple, while it is freely used today for normal places of Christian worship. William' translation reads as follows in the old English: "For ye have brought hyther these me whiche are nether robbers of churches nor yet despisers of youre goddes." From: http://wesley.nnu.edu/biblical_studies/tyndale/Tyndale.pdf

Even from William's Tyndale's translation is clear that the word Church or Churches was associate with pagan temples and the Greek word Ecclesia when applied to believers was always translated either as "assembly" or "congregation" of Ysra'el.

It's clear to any who can see YHWH never had any Contracts with a pagan temple system or churches. Even modern churches that are married to paganism have no Contract with YHWH as they do not teach his full law. YHWH does not acknowledge them as truth bearers.

Even their singing is seen as noise by YHWH that they claim to be worshipping the holy one of Y'sra'el.

> **Amos 5:23** Take away from me the noise of your songs; for I will not hear the melody of your stringed instruments.

YHWH only ever acknowledged one family which was Y'sra'el and remains to be so.

> **Amos 3:2** You only have I known of all the families of the earth:[8] therefore I will punish you for all your iniquities.

Did YHWH ever say he acknowledges Contracts/Agreements with an entity called a Church? No, and never can it stand while it stands Torahless or better known as lawless.

Who are the Real Hebrews?

So who is real Ysra'el the present people in the land or someone completely different?

If I asked any of you that has Y'sra'el been recreated many of you will be more than happy to say yes in 1948. If I pressed you hard to show me a prophecy that says Y'sra'el was recreated you may go to the book of Yeshayahu (Isaiah) and show me the following verse.

> **Yeshayahu (Isa) 66:8** Who has heard such a thing? Who has seen such things? Shall the earth be made to bring forth in one day? Or shall a nation be born at once?[9] For as soon as Tsiyon travailed, she brought forth her children.

---

[8] YHWH only knows Y'sra'el and no other family, any church that is not engrafted and in sync with Y'sra'el has no place in the world to come.

[9] The rebirth of Israel that will bring forth the twelve tribes to return yet not completely fulfilled.

If I then asked you have the Ysraelites returned you will be glad to tell me of course just look over at Y'sra'el. Then if I asked you where did these masses returned from. You will be so excited to tell me from Europe and Russia just as the Bible said. Now I ask you please show me where it says in the bible that the first returnees are from Europe and Russia.

This may give you pause thinking to search in the scriptures. Ah now things become a little bit trickier. I also tell you that the prophecy you just cited earlier does not fit with the return of 1948 you get a little taken aback. You retort why? It is very simple that you have likely learnt this stuff from some messianic or Christian assembly and have never really looked into the bible to verify these things for yourself for context or sat with a teacher knowledgeable enough to guide you why things cannot just be applied randomly out of the bible to fit our worldview. That is what normally Christians do.

It's also clear that you do not understand that when Y'sra'el came into being in 1948 there were a lot of people in the Arab side murdered and evicted from their homes. A lot of people who subsequently went to Y'sra'el or supported Y'sra'el and its state. It was the Rothschild's (Red Shield) the German bankers who used their unrighteous wealth to bring Y'sra'el as a nation through the British with political lobbying. So are we saying that Elohim is responsible for sin and allows unrighteous wealth to bring his kingdom together? Is murder no longer sin? Then what about the murder of Palestinians in the land? Is usury no longer sin, which is how the Rothschild's have been earning their money since the 18th century by putting the world into debt?

Should we just ignore these matters and treat this like a war where anyone can be killed but in a war when people are killed usually they have guns to fight back but the Arab men and children who were lined up from ten to fifty years of age had no guns. They were told to march towards Jordan; if they refused then they were shot. Does this sound like Palestinians leaving their homes voluntarily when villages were systematically depopulated one by one, another lie branded by the Zionists that the Palestinians left their homes voluntarily. Their homes were bombed and forcefully evacuated. Does all this sound like right-ruling war? Perhaps the Palestinians are just rats and spiders which can just be squashed under foot, their women, children can just be randomly picked off while walking in streets and shot and killed. Is this not the same attitude Hitler carried over these Zionist Europeans? And they act the same to other foreigners in the land. Yet even the Palestinians who wanted to remain in pace would have fared much better under Moses.

> **Shemoth 22:21** You shall neither mistreat a foreigner nor oppress him, for you were foreigners in the land of Mitzrayim (Egypt).

The homes of Palestinians have been demolished at the whims and desires of the likes of Benjamin Netanyahu. What you sow you will reap. The time for this unrighteous nation and its judgment is looming and it's a matter of time before YHWH unleashes His judgment. If no repentance is come forth then no one can stop the judgment for the cleansing that will go forth into this land first before the real Y'sraelites are taken back and the illegal immigrants, the Zionists removed from the land. Only those will remain that Yahuweh sees fit according to His will.

> Reported by the Independent
> **Pro-Palestinian 'flytilla' stopped at airports by Israeli security By Catrina Stewart in Jerusalem**
>
> *Saturday, 9 July 2011*

Israel detained dozens of pro-Palestinian activists yesterday at its main airport and deterred hundreds more from boarding flights to Israel in a security operation ridiculed by domestic media as excessive.

In the second mass event protesting Israel's policies towards Palestinians in as many weeks, up to 800 rights campaigners had hoped to land in Tel Aviv yesterday and declare their intention to travel to the occupied West Bank to try to expose Israeli restrictions on access to the Palestinian territory.

Israel largely thwarted those plans after issuing foreign airlines with a blacklist of more than 340 people compiled from social media sites. It urged the airlines to prevent the activists from boarding, warning them that they would bear the cost of flying them back. Most of those who did make it onto their flights – at least 55 – were stopped at Israeli immigration and faced deportation.

The boats were sabotaged by the Y'sraelite secret police in Greece and Turkey while both Greece and Turkey took part in the unrighteous actions with Y'sra'el. Or maybe it was the swordfish that put their long snout in the propellers and broke them. The swordfish must have been working under cover to attack at the same time.

Yet these people have the audacity to say that they are a democracy. Yahuweh wants a theocracy and not a demolition demo-kretinacy that is leading people to destruction. One can understand that when Gog and Magog attack Y'sra'el part of the Gog-turks are already in the land pretending to be Y'sraelites. These will also be flushed by Yahuweh (Ezek 38:1, 22).

Israel rejects allegations it sabotaged Gaza flotilla ships
By Barak Ravid and The Associated Press

Israel has denied claims it sabotaged ships trying to breach its naval blockade of the Gaza Strip.

Activists have accused Israel of damaging two ships docked in Turkey and Greece that are part of a flotilla attempting to reach the Palestinian territory with humanitarian aid.

Y'sra'el has become nothing but a bully state in the east and the nations see it the same way. No one today sees Y'sra'el as the nation that was meant to give light unto the world. **HOW CAN THEY GIVE LIGHT THAT DON'T HAVE ANY SINCE THEY ARE ALL EURO FOREIGNERS ILLEGAL OCCUPANTS IN THE LAND TRYING TO FORCE THE KINGDOM OF YAH THINKING THEY HAVE SOME KIND OF RIGHT from the HEAVENS, THEY DON'T!!!**

You can argue all day and praise them but the unrighteous state of Y'sra'el is just that today as it was in 1948 when it was created with unrighteous wealth. In fact things have gotten worse.

Y'sra'el today is the homosexual capital of the middle-east where homosexual men feel safe and go to look for refuge. Did Elohim not command to eliminate sodomy from the land? Would that not then mean that any type of homosexuality has to be banned in the land and those who are of this inclination removed? See what many are doing? In their ignorance they blaspheme YHWH and attribute sin to him. Do You suggest that Elohim created Y'sra'el in sin? This is what all of those who proclaim Y'sra'el have been doing. How foolish of them.

We cannot just dodge the issue. The second issue is of Muslims and their mosques in the land. If this was really Yahuweh's recreation then why were the mosques not removed from the land immediately? Why was the Temple mount not cleansed? You may be forgiven for making the excuse that in 1948 the Zionists were not strong enough to do that but what about in 1967 when they were strong enough? The evidence is pretty clear that Y'sra'el's present recreation is by the hands of men, the claim to the land by the European Zionists is false but it was allowed to stand simply because the persecution they faced in the German holocaust. The nations felt an injustice had been done so they voted for the land to be given to these men. These men and women are gentiles and not of true Y'sraelite stock but that is another dilemma that many of you need to resolve. You also need to answer how a white race ended up in a black land!

From these facts alone one is clear that Christians and Zionists have come to some very faulty conclusions without any understanding of what has been proposed is simply impossible. This is not a denial of the fact that Y'sra'el as a secular state does not exist on the contrary it does. It did come into existence via all the necessary secular channels but that does not give it credibility as a state recreated by YHWH. It is foolish to say that YHWH needed the vote of nations to recreate His state. Did he need the vote of nations in Egypt to remove his people from bondage?

Now to look at the prophecy in Isaiah 66:8 if it was true for 1948 and I will categorically tell you it cannot be applied to 1948. A land created in sin cannot have the right-ruling hands of Elohim upon it. A right-ruling Elohim can allow sin to continue until a time He no longer will tolerate it but we cannot attribute sin to him.

Am I the only one to ask these questions and see that things don't seem to fit? Maybe you do not see things as I do but that is OK however now I am putting you on the stand and asking you to reexamine your stance based on the evidences I have presented of what a right-ruling state should look like or even the beginnings of a right-ruling state.

> **Yeshayahu (Isa) 66:12** For thus says YHWH, Behold, I will extend shalom (peace) to her like a river, and the glory of the Gentiles like a flowing stream: then shall you suck, you shall be borne upon her sides, and be dandled upon her knees.

Now if the 1948 prophecy was a fulfillment for Yeshayahu (Isa) 66:8 then how are we going to answer the verse in Yeshayahu 66:12? This says when Yeshayahu 66:8 comes to pass then <u>peace</u> MUST follow! That the glory of the Gentiles will follow with worship in Jerusalem by the gentiles. Has peace followed? No. We have seen six wars in that region and we will see more to come.

It's clear both the Zionists and Christians have cajoled each other and created a myth in their heads of a state that is ordained by man and not the Most High. They can both clap for each other while the real Y'sra'elites are still dispersed outside the land and are awaiting rescue in the future from the nations they are in. When that happens then the whole world will see the Biblical state of Y'sra'el being reborn. Right now we have all the east European gentiles gathered together in Y'sra'el who proclaim a homeland by force and coercing the nations with unrighteous wealth of bankers like Rothschild's.

Many people have got it fixed in their head that the present day Jews mainly Caucasians are the true Hebrews therefore anytime you try to show people that the majority of these are not the true Semitic people is met with opposition and even aggression at times. Why such opposition?

Some people have come and asked me questions about the variety of Jews in the world such as the varying Judaism' what really is a true Hebrew and who is not by ancient definition?

There are three main groupings of Jews in the world today as follows:

Middle-Eastern
Ashkenazi
Sephardic

First of all the majority of the Ashkenazi today are not Semitic so anytime anyone says anything against them while Christians will try to defend this "with do not curse the Jews or you will be cursed" without even understanding what they are saying is not true for just anyone claiming to be part of the ancient tribe of Yahudah (Judah).

This is only true for Shem or Shemitic people these were the sons of Abraham which were Shemetic, while many today claim to be the sons of Abraham are Japhetic and not Shemetic.

Why did I just say sons and not son?

This is because the churches largely corrupted theology that Isaac is the only Hebrew and the rest of the sons of Abraham are not is a fallacy which I shall just prove.

Abraham was married to Keturah his wife in the south living in Beersheba in Israel in ancient times and she was the daughter of Joktan who was the son of Shem. So then by definition would her sons which were black and the leading progenitors of the Arab races be classed as Shemitic or non-Shemitic? Joktan mentioned in Genesis 10:25 is the First real pure Arab and He predates the birth of Yahudah Jacob's son by 100s of years. He was the first

Arab Hebrew because his Daddy was Eber the first Hebrew and Keturah Abraham's wife was his daughter. They were people of colour.

Her sons are as follows:

> **Genesis 25:2** And she had birthed him Zimran, Yokshan, Medan, Midian, Ishvak, and Shuah.

These are the real progenitors of the Arab people, who inhabited the eastern Arabian Peninsula so do the Arabs have the right to be in the land of Israel today or do Europeans claiming to be the sons of Shem have the right, while the majority of them are actually the sons of Japheth? Who is the real owner of that land many are fighting over today?

This also means that not any Tom, Dick and Harry in Israel today can just make a claim and own the land what many have done. Another disturbing report came from Israel that they were trying to wipe out the black race of Yahudim living amongst them. These are the hated one's the Ethiopian Yahudim many of which are known as Falashas. This case alleges that a very potent drug is given to the black Ethiopian Ysraelites to suppress them having children and can at time render the women infertile for months as a birth control.

Please see the video below.

http://rt.com/news/ethiopian-women-contraceptive-infertility/

These black Yahudim by the way are the real sons of King Solomon from the tribe of Yahudah which are today given birth control medication to the women that can make them sterile and even cause irreparable damage to their bodies while they are not told of the dangers. The interesting thing is that this particular drug is banned in many European states and in Israel this drug is not prescribed to any Caucasian Jew. Now read between the lines. Also I want to make one thing crystal clear so that you do not venture into a wrong understanding. There are Caucasian Jews today who are the sons of Shem, however we have to separate the wheat from the Chaff but that requires another detailed study because they are few in number.

Some brave Caucasian Jews in Israel have blown the cover on the State's use of such medication which is being given without any guidance of its side-effects to the black community. This could be conceived as nothing short of what Hitler was doing with the Jews in the 40s when he also experimented with them through his doctors.

Some of us may see the parallels while others may not.

For all practical purposes and identification the majority Ashkenazi are not the true sons of Shem while there is a minority that is related to Shem. This is because anyone in the Ashkenazi majority honestly trace his lineage would find his Turkish roots. That is correct because the sons of Japheth ended up in Turkey followed by them living in Russia and around Russia where the Khazars converted into Judaism. The 15 CIS states of Russia are all Turkic. Turkic people even can be found in China.

This majority of the formal European Jewry was at one time living near the Caspian Sea and were residents of a kingdom called Khazaria in the 8th century CE.

If you would like to read more about this then you should get the book written by a well known historian of the 20th century called Arthur Koestler who was Jewish who can show you proof by proof the origins of the people who called themselves Ashkenazi today and how this majority came to live in Europe from the break up of the Khazari kingdom near Russia. His book is called The 13th Tribe. These subsequently inhabited Poland (where large Jewish families are from). Also note the original Jews or Yahudim in Europe were massacred and they only numbered in the hundreds and not thousands long before the holocaust. The reason why the later Ashkenazi who took on the identity of the earlier Jews and their religion received similar treatment of pogroms and even the holocaust is because they identified themselves with the Yahudit religion called Judaism and practices of Hebrew Israelites.

If you look in Israel today some of these people are so cold with the typical Russian look. As an exercise I encourage you to engage a Russian in conversation, then engage a British and engage an American with the same types of conversation. You will find out of these the ones with an indifferent look is the Russian while both the British and American are quite happy to talk about anything till the cows go home. Note also that the Khazari people had many converts who went to Ukraine, Belarus and Kiev. They also helped establish the Hungarian script; many Hungarian Jews are also of Khazari origin. They inhabited Poland in large numbers.

So in essence Hitler's holocaust was really directed against <u>East</u> Europeans who he ignorantly thought were the sons of Shem simply because they identified themselves with the faith of our real forefathers. There is no doubt in my mind that some people who were killed by him were the Sephardic Jews who were the sons of Shem and they were lighters skinned or Caucasian. What most do not know is that this was all a conspiracy by the so called Zionists who by the way are not after Elohim or his Torah. They were political and a political movement to acquire land first in Uganda which failed then they managed to secure land in Israel and call it their home. They perpetrated the holocaust and had massive number of Jews killed so that they could get sympathy vote. They did not always hide their agenda as you will learn here.

We even know through the annals of history that many of these eastern European Jews could have been saved but were slaughtered because it was expedient as the Zionists knew that the more that die the better it is for them to claim a homeland in Israel since they had previously failed to get a place in Uganda. Hitler had offered to send all the Jews to Spain but no one will ever tell you that so why hide this history?

Because it pays to beat on the same old drum that we are the victims of the holocaust. A good book to read on the victim theology is one of a very good author called Beyond Chutzpah by Norman Finklestien who is also Jewish. His book the Holocaust Industry is a real eye opener and this man is a history professor and knows his stuff well. He has defeated such Zionists as Alan Dershowitz and has featured on numerous TV interviews that the Zionist media will not want you to see.

http://www.normanfinkelstein.com/

I respect this man greatly for his in-depth knowledge of the historical situation in Israel and the two sides of the conflict. I encourage you to listen to him. When he exposed Zionism for the evil that it is then the Zionists lobby had him removed from his university job and accused him of all sorts of wrongs that he did not commit yet this man is also Jewish. Even if you are Jewish and you speak against the evils of Zionism they will turn against you and I guarantee you that this has happened to Jews of all people this is simply because the Zionists love money and serve mammon so don't be fooled. I do not support any Zionists organization in America nor in Israel and would prohibit any of you to do so because we are forbidden to join ranks with those who do not advocate the bringing in of Torah government. We do not care how much cash they wad around but they are politically motivated and racists at best. We live in the West with the illusion of democracies but are really controlled by governments and individuals who run the show behind the scenes.

Remember YHWH called us Zion his daughter (Ps 9:14; Lam 1:6; Zec 2:10) and its really a term for Israel and Jerusalem in the narrower context and I see it like that and not like controlling and manipulating markets and banks that mostly are involved in and overthrowing democratic or despotic governments of the world, that is not our business and we should steer clear of such ideas.

So now tell me what is the difference between living in a Muslim country that throws you in jail or worse kills you for standing against Islamic ideology versus political Zionism? Actually the line is very thin for those of you who think I am joking joining the two look what happened to Noman Finklestien who was removed from his job and not employed or allowed to be employed later. Does that sound like democracy or a police state covered with an illusion of democracy? It's time to take that green pill to see things more clearly.

The political Zionists are responsible for the holocaust and supporters of it. They have blood on their hands of over twelve million people and YHWH will judge them one day. I know it maybe painful for some of you to learn this truth but I encourage you to ask Yahushua our Master to bring shalom and understanding in your hearts and lives. I discourage all Black Hebrews who advocate hating the white man ideology and do not support such notions. One man's wrong does not allow us to condemn the whole white race. We must learn to forgive and make peace with ourselves and others. Notice what scripture says:

> **Matthew 5:9** Increased are the shalom (peace) makers[10] for they shall be called the children of Elohim.

So if you want to see the face of our Elohim we must strive for peace.

The Zionist camp knew that if they had accepted the transference of all Jewry into Spain then they will not get the land of Israel so they refused to accept this. It was said by them that a cow of Palestine is worth more than all the Jews of Poland or even Europe depending on who you believe. Now you decide if a cow is worth more than over twelve million human lives? These twelve million included six million Jews, nineteen thousand Catholic Priests, Six million Christians, thirty five thousand Gypsies and countless Blacks that are never mentioned. Some suggest 50,000 blacks but I would suggest this figure is wrong. We also must never forget the black holocaust of slavery that displaced 26 million black people. Sin has a price and the Black Hebrews paid it.

For those of you who still doubt that the black Negro race are Hebrews here is what Zondervan publisher say with their own mouths and they are white folks:

> Zondervan's Compact Bible Dictionary listed under Ham it defines as such: The youngest son of Noah, born probably about 96 years before the Flood; and one of eight persons to live through the Flood. He became the progenitor of the dark races; **NOT THE NEGROES**, but the Egyptians, Ethiopians, Libyans and Canaanites.

---

[10] This was for those who wanted to live out the life of Torah obedience echoing Psalm 34:14.

So they admit with a stiff upper lip but they do admit it and make no other clarifications. However you will find all the clarifications in the Hidden-Truths Hebraic Scrolls study Bible where no Bible even comes close to its interpretation and commentary from www.african-israel.com.

Here is the quotation for your references.

[11]Izaak Greenbaum -- head of Jewish Agency Rescue Committee February 18, 1943

Addressed to the Zionist Executive Council.

"One Cow in Palestine is worth more than all the Jews in Poland"

....Izaak Greenbaum

Here is what the first president of Israel thought of the old people in Europe.

"The old ones will pass. They will bear their fate or they will not."

---

[11] http://www.jewsagainstzionism.com/antisemitism/holocaust/index.cfm

Chaim Weizmann, the first president of Israel, made this Zionist policy very explicit: The hopes of Europe's six million Jews are centered on emigration. I was asked: "Can you bring six million Jews to Palestine?" I replied, "No." ... From the depths of the tragedy I want to save ... young people [for Palestine]. The old ones will pass. They will bear their fate or they will not. They are dust, economic and moral dust in a cruel world ... Only the branch of the young shall survive. They have to accept it.

Chaim Weizmann reporting to the Zionist Congress in 1937 on his testimony before the Peel Commission in London, July 1937. Cited in Yahya, p. 55. Ben Gurion informed a meeting of Labor Zionists in Great Britain in 1938: "If I knew that it would be possible to save all the children in Germany by bringing them over to England and only half of them by transporting them to Eretz Israel, then I opt for the second alternative." Ibid., p.149.

As late as 1943, while the Jews of Europe were being exterminated in their millions, the U.S. Congress proposed to set up a commission to "study" the problem. Rabbi Stephen Wise, who was the principal American spokesperson for Zionism, came to Washington to testify against the rescue bill because it would divert attention from the colonization of Palestine.

This is the same Rabbi Wise who, in 1938, in his capacity as leader of the American Jewish Congress, wrote a letter in which he opposed any change in U.S. immigration laws which would enable Jews to find refuge. He stated:

"It may interest you to know that some weeks ago the representatives of all the leading Jewish organizations met in conference ... It was decided that no Jewish organization would, at this time, sponsor a bill which would in any way alter the immigration laws."

This is clear cut proof that the political Zionists were quite happy for the masses in Europe to be slaughtered for a greater cause that was to get the land.

So then what about the increases they are receiving today in Israel?

Well since many of these were converts into Judaism they started to keep the Torah and it is a proof in itself that those who obey the Torah no matter whether black or white, yellow or green, sons of Shem or sons of Japheth they would receive the benefits. This only goes to prove the power of the Torah of what Elohim has declared beforehand. While the true sons of Shem the people of colour were sent into exile and others who were not were receiving the benefits and it is as simple as that. This does not mean YHWH changed his mind and decided to give the land to Japheth. The land is given to them for an appointed time only. I have illustrated this in my final volume of the World war III – part 4 "The second Exodus," what will happen to these people and what signs should we be looking at.

We need to understand two more things. Judaism has been preserved by the Ashkenazi and Sephardic people and without these two today we would not have a Torah, the Tanak or how to keep the feasts so we must be careful not to just write everyone off as I see many Hebrew Israelites doing.

The Sephardic community

The Sephardic community of Jews many which do carry the blood of Shem, they are mix of white, pale white or very light brown skin colour but these Yahudi are one of the branches of the sons of Shem. Although the true Hebrew Israelites were black people but these people came out of what I define as the mix of black Hebrews with European or Asian women in Egypt. Where did these Asians come from? They came from Asia invading Egypt and they were captured and even thrown out at one time then they were made slaves and eventually they were released and allowed to take citizenship in Egypt which is where we find the mixing happened.

It is well known historically that Egypt where the majority Hebrews lived were invaded by the Asian people in lower Egypt through the sea and land. The invading Asians were of course people of very light skin and since these people mixed with the Hebrews living in the land during their captivity they obviously are then likely to produce Asian skin tones. Note White or pale white is an Asian skin tone and these people are known as Cauc-Asians.

Our witness that many Sephardic are really the sons of Shem can also come from Arthur Koestler in which Hasdai Ibn Shaprut a Sephardic Yahudi living in Spain wrote to the king of Khazaria called Joseph enquiring of the mass conversions there by the local white folks.

> The 13th Tribe page 25 by Arthur Koestler
> This is the so-called "Khazar Correspondence": an exchange of letters, in Hebrew, between Hasdai Ibn Shaprut, the Jewish chief minister of the Caliph of Cordoba, and Joseph, King of the Khazars or, rather, between their respective scribes. The authenticity of the correspondence has been the subject of controversy but is now generally accepted with due allowance made for the vagaries of later copyists. [A summary of the controversy will be found in Appendix III.]
>
> The exchange of letters apparently took place after 954 and before 961 that is roughly at the time when Masudi wrote. To appreciate its significance a word

must be said about the personality of Hasdai Ibn Shaprut – perhaps the most brilliant figure in the "Golden Age" (900-1200) of the Jews in Spain.

IBID Page 28
I feel the urge to know the truth, whether there is really a place on this earth where harassed Israel can rule itself, where it is subject to nobody. If I were to know that this is indeed the case, I would not hesitate to forsake all honours, to resign my high office, to abandon my family, and to travel over mountains and plains, over land and water, until I arrived at the place where my Lord, the [Jewish] King rules . . . And I also have one more request: to be informed whether you have any knowledge of [the possible date] of the Final Miracle [the coming of the Messiah] which, wandering from country to country, we are awaiting. Dishonoured and humiliated in our dispersion, we have to listen in silence to those who say: "every nation has its own land and you alone possess not even a shadow of a country on this earth".

IBID page 29-30
We have our eyes on the sages of Jerusalem and Babylon, and although we live far away from Zion, we have nevertheless heard that the calculations are erroneous owing to the great profusion of sins, and we know nothing, only the Eternal knows how to keep the count. We have nothing to hold on only the prophecies of Daniel, and may the Eternal speed up our Deliverance . . .

There is a passage in Joseph's letter which deals with topical politics, and is rather obscure: *With the help of the Almighty I guard the mouth of the river [the Volga] and do not permit the Rus who come in their ships to invade the land of the Arabs ... I fight heavy wars with them [the Rus] for if I allowed it they would devastate the lands of Ishmael even to Baghdad.* Joseph here appears to pose as the defender of the Baghdad Caliphate against the Norman-Rus raiders (see Chapter III). This might seem a little tactless in view of the bitter hostility between the Omayad Caliphate of Cordoba (which

Hasdai is serving) and the Abassid Caliphs of Baghdad. On the other hand, the vagaries of Byzantine policy towards the Khazars made it expedient for Joseph to appear in the role of a defender of Islam, regardless of the schism between the two Caliphates. At least he could hope that Hasdai, the experienced diplomat, would take the hint.

He does mention, however, that while he was in Baghdad, he had seen envoys from the Khazar kingdom looking for needy Jewish scholars from Mesopotamia and even from Egypt, "to teach their children Torah and Talmud".

Who were the Khazars?

> Ibid page 7
> But before becoming a sovereign state, the Khazars still had to serve their apprenticeship under another short-lived power, the so-called West Turkish Empire, or Turkut kingdom. It was a confederation of tribes, held together by a ruler: the Kagan or Khagan (Or Kaqan or Khaqan or Chagan, etc. Orientalists have strong Idiosyncrasies about spelling [see Appendix I]. I shall stick to Kagan as the least offensive to Western eyes. The h in Khazar, however, is general usage), – a title which the Khazar rulers too were subsequently to adopt. This first Turkish state – if one may call it that – lasted for a century (circa 550-650) and then fell apart, leaving hardly any trace. However, it was only after the establishment of this kingdom that the name "Turk" was used to apply to a specific nation, as distinct from other Turkic-speaking peoples like the Khazars and Bulgars. (This, however, did not prevent the name "Turk" still being applied indiscriminately to any nomadic tribe of the steppes as a euphemism for Barbarian

These sons of Japheth which are the Turks.

> **Genesis 10:2** The sons of Yapheth were Gomer, Magog (Turkey), Madai, Yavan, Tubal, Meshech (Turkey), and Tiras.

Now we can answer the question who the majority Ashkenazi are. They are actually Turkish and do not have a drop of Shem's blood. One would have to lie to prove that they did. However from the previous discourses between Hasdai a leading physician in the court of the Muslim Caliph in Cordoba in Spain it is evident that these ones (Sephardic) were indeed the sons of Shem as explained their lighter colouring would come from the mixing. Note some European Jews were the sons of Shem but they were very small in number like on the hundreds.

Now what about the middle-Eastern Jewry?

It is also a historical fact that there was a whole kingdom that converted into Judaism in Yemen. In 500 AD, the King of Himyar, Abu-Kariba Assad alongside his whole kingdom converted into Judaism thus rejecting both Christianity and Zoroastrian religion of Iran which had the influence in that region. This is a very important testimony to show that **pagan Christianity** was rejected by those who understood it well even at that time since this was a creation of the Roman Catholic Church and her corrupt councils in the year 325 AD onwards. Original people living in these lands of Yemen were the sons of Shem the son of Joktan, the first pure Arab who was black so they rightfully chose their true faith which means they are the true sons of Shem.

Let me show you.

> **Genesis 10:25-30** To Eber were born two sons: the name of one was Peleg;[12] for in his days the earth was divided; and his brother's name was Yoktan. **26** Yoktan[13] begot Almodad, Sheleph, Hazarmaveth, Yerah, **27** Hadoram, Uzal, Diklah, **28** Obal, Abimael, Sheba,[14] **29** Ophir,[15] Chavilah,

---

[12] A city near the Euphrates called Phalga.

[13] The ancestor of the southern Arabs called Qahtan.

[14] Sheba was black inhabiting regions of Africa.

[15] Ophir is the biblical term for the land of Africa noting that the term 'Africa' is of late historical derivative. In the Greek tongue the term Frike means cold and horror and appending the A to it becomes Africa which mean "not the land of cold and horror" but as can be seen many horrors were perpetrated there by the so called civilised nations of the

and Yobab: all these were the sons of Yoktan. **30** And their dwelling place was from Mesha,[16] as you go toward Sephar, the mountain of the east.[17]

Note Yoktan's sons' occupied regions both in Eastern Arabia and some as far North as Africa and Western Africa. Some of Yoktan's sons ruled as Kings for a thousand years in Yemen.

Chavilah one name covers regions both in Arabia and West Africa which is mentioned in the Bible as Havilah (Gen 2:11). Since Yoktan was Shem's son therefore one can prove that those people in Yemen opting for Judaism was nothing short of a call from Elohim. Mesha (Gen 10:30) is also the old name for the Meccan region of Saudi Arabia mentioned in Scripture.

We also know from Islamic historical sources that the Yahudim lived in Saudi Arabia and in other Islamic countries. One other thing that bears out by later Muslims is that they also knew that the Yahudim lived in Black lands of Africa which once again is testimony that many Hebrew Israelites were living there prior to the slave trade when many of these same people were brought into Europe and America. I am a living testimony of my forefathers who were taken as captives to Iran later after my forefather's freedom they were extremely wealthy merchants from the Levite tribe.

What about the Khazars?

They were also converted into Judaism rather than into Christianity as they also say Christianity as pagan and also rejected Islam because of the hand of Elohim was upon them. This may be hard to swallow for some but this is the truth because a prophecy was given that they would be enticed/deceived into believing that they are the sons of Shem.

---

world one such as slavery and colonization to subjugate the 10,000 kingdoms that existed there. In the Latin language the term Afrika meant sunny. It is well known that India's and China's ancestors were African people and also they were the early inhabitants of the Americas.

[16] Ancient name for Mecca in Western-Saudi Arabia.
[17] Pilgrimage place of Islam.

Genesis 9:27 Elohim will deceive Yapheth, and he will dwell in the tents of Shem; and may Canaan be his servant

The word for deceive which in the King James Version is <u>enlarge</u>. The actually meaning of the Hebrew word is to <u>deceive</u> so much so that they will not only occupy the houses of Shem but believe that they are Shem!!!! Is this true today? Yes.

In fact it is YHWH who deceived the Caucasian Europeans through the evil one that they will think they are the chosen ones when they in fact are not. They will go and take over the land of Y'sra'el as their own which has already happened. Patah in Hebrew means to speak evil from the heart but show a different face in other words two faced. Many European leaders will be two faced in the End of Days when they are deceived by their own minds and the people who reject YHWH will fall into lewdness see Romans chapter 1.18-32. However the door would be open for good Caucasian people to join our people to serve YHWH that they may be rescued from the end-times wrath.

Today the true Y'sra'elites are not in the land of Y'sra'el but many Ashkenazim Hebrews are in fact converts from the kingdom of Khazar. They are not Semitic but in fact are the sons of Yapheth. Just as YHWH had said they will occupy the tents of Shem and will look like Shem so they do today likewise. However in the future a time will come when the original Black Hebrews will be brought into Y'sra'el and Yapheth removed to his proper place. According to letters sent and received by the Sephardic Yahudim the King of Khazaria who was Yosef himself said they had descended from Yapheth. Note also after the breakup of the kingdom they all ended in modern Western Europe from where many of these migrated into Y'sra'el claiming to be ancient Yahudim. They are not.

> The 13th Tribe p28 by Arthur Koestler
> Eldad visited Spain around 880 and may or may not have visited the Khazar country. Hasdai briefly mentions him in his letter to Joseph – as if to ask what to make of him. Joseph then proceeds to provide a genealogy of his people. Though a fierce

Hebrew nationalist, proud of wielding the 'sceptre of Judah", he cannot, and does not, claim for them Semitic descent; he traces their ancestry not to Shem, but to Noah's third son, Japheth;

Very few people in ancient Y'sra'el are from the Yahudim stock that is the Sephardic, African and Persian Jewry alone make up that stock while the Ashkanaz are really East European Khazar converts into Judaism.

Today the white Ashkenazi Jews believe they are Shem while we know they are not. Noah's prophecy said they will dwell in the tents (read Houses) of Shem. Today they occupy the land of Israel just as predicted. However a time will come when YHWH will sort out the right order when the true children some of which are already in Israel as illustrated earlier such as the black Yahudim, the middle-eastern Yahudim and perhaps some Ashkenazim who are the real sons of Shem while large parts of the twelve tribes still remain outside Israel.

A lot more can be said but hopefully now you start to get the picture. I will give you the complete picture of the return when I complete my book later this year which will explain step by step what is going to happen and how YHWH will take us back to our inheritance so don't pack your bags and don't even worry about how it will happen.

I assure you everything is in YHWH's hands. One testimony to encourage those of you who have been following some groups who advocate packing your bags so to speak maybe sometimes literally ignore them.

I was a Muslim for 35 years of my life until 1998 September I did not know that I was a Hebrew let alone an Israelite. I did not even know the connections of my forefathers being Iranian Yahudi until Yahushua suddenly out of nowhere called me out while working in a major Japanese merchant bank called Nomura in London spoke to me to "follow Him." I knew nothing, no bible theology, I had never touched a bible in my life until then but then He started to unfold the plan step by step. The first thing he did was show the annual festivals to me and forbid me to celebrate Christmas and Easter pagan feasts. Then He taught me the weekly Sabbaths and how to do them so my preliminary training with him took six years.

Some people have asked me how do you know that we are Black Hebrews and that why do you teach it. I will attest to you that I know a lot more than I attest to and I follow the good advice of my friend Rabbi Ariel in Israel who was a Lubavitcher Rabbi and before he became a believer, he told me not to reveal everything to the people. Some things that the Most High YHWH has revealed to me many are hard truths that the people will laugh at and ridicule me about so I follow that advice to only reveal in part. There are things that I know but I cannot reveal and there are things that I must reveal when Yahushua tells me to, no matter even it breaks me or my family. Sometimes I hint other times I declare clearly that is how things are. I have spoken about this truth before, in fact hinted at it more than once even on Revelation TV and called myself clearly an Israelite, I doubt even many understood the term.

My son little Yosef Halewi who was born on Feb 2nd the boy YHWH promised me and for whom I was ridiculed, laughed at and called demon possessed and delirious by some foolish Christians, my own ex-wife not only divorced me but helped to slander me through others but I remained silent. YHWH has his time set for judgment for all these people, vengeance is His.

Muslims on the other hand said noting against me and gave me respect, invited me to their homes and even to their mosque while I was cut off by the so called Christian community but I refused to enter another church that teach anti-Torah doctrines and pagan philosophy.

There was a conspiracy made against me by some Zionist Christians to destroy me but they failed miserably, their slander of me only made my resolve stronger and out of all this was produced the AFN Study bible. Can you imagine a Bible emerging from the Chaos and hypocrisy around me. It indeed happened and a day is not far when I will see justice. Those believers who were sincere and close to me saw first hand the hypocrisy of the Zionist Christian community too.

I simply went to my bedroom and prayed to YHWH on my sheepskin mat for justice while I gave over their judgment to YHWH asking that he see their hypocrisy and judge them on his part for the breaking of Torah.

So naturally such people should take note their time is now short for judgment unless repentance comes the rod will fall. These are what I term hypocritical Christians with so called ministries and websites that people should steer clear of. They espouse hatred of Muslims and I will not stand with them to condemn the many sons of Shem that one day will see the light of Yahushua.

The Hebrew marriage removed and replaced by the Greco/Roman model

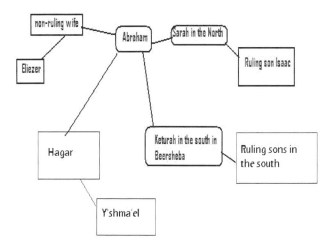

Abraham had four wives listed as follows as a Patriarch:

1 Keturah
2 Sarah
3 Mashek
4 Hagar

Sara was the name of an African tribe so Sarah was titled Sar-i, Abraham's wife was his half sister/cousin/patrilineal niece but she was given the title Sara which later was changed by YHWH to Sara-h by appending the h (in

Hebrew the heh Character) she became Sar-ah. It was common custom and is still common custom in Hebrews and even in Islam that is strictly followed in the Muslims today to marry patrilineal nieces or cousins. My younger brother who is still a Muslim is married to my and his patrilineal niece. There is nothing wrong with it and it is perfectly acceptable according to the Torah to marry your patrilineal niece or cousin. One example in the Bible where a niece is married to her uncle is the famous story of Ruth and Boaz. Ruth's mother-in-law Naomi was EliMelek's niece and he was her uncle and she was married to him.

In ancient Hebrew the name Sarah does not mean a "princess", this is only in rabbinic modernism applying modern tenants of the modern Hebrew language. Today's Hebrew is nothing like the ancient Hebrew and true ancient Hebrew has not been revived yet fully!

In Ancient script the letters Sin (S), Resh (R) and Yud (Y) meant "A bright distinguished Bird." Note in the ancient Egyptian culture it was very common to see birds, cats, dogs, and other such animals as symbols. The same is actually true in ancient Hebrew but since it was lost to the Hebrew people more research needs to be done in this area. Also in ancient Iraq (Babylon) the lion was a common symbol. Each culture had its special ancient symbols.

Abraham's wife Sarah was a fair black woman hence the term/title etc plus she was the ruling matriarch in her tribe. Many questions arise from the text in Genesis. If Abraham was already married to Keturah and had children at fifty then why does Abraham say "I remain childless" (Gen 15:2) in the translation of the King James Version of the text? How come the scholars have never addressed this seeming issue?

The real Hebrew language was a monosyllable language just like the Egyptian script and did not originally have two or three letter roots in its makeup while this is simply the development of Hebrew from the ancient cultures. The second letter or the third letter only gave more meaning to the first letter so whenever you decipher an Ancient Hebrew word always look at the first character. The meaning is embedded in that. Here is a prime example.

The Letter Yod, Yud or Yeh, 👁 it is the picture of an eye. So what would be the meaning of this ancient character on its own?

The idea of the all Seeing Eye is not new but very ancient. The meaning would be simply the opposite of not seeing. So if we can see what do we have? We have the meaning of LIGHT, VISION, and BRIGHTNESS. However if we cannot see then we have darkness, un-illumined, and no vision. These are binary opposites. The ancient Hebrews were of a binary culture. Light/Dark, Sun/Moon, Earth/Sky, Man/Woman and hot/cold, etc. Hence the meaning of the Yud is "LIGHT." Did Yahushua declare anything of this? Yes. So those of you who have a hard time with how can he be God, it is embedded in the Yud and He declared it. He operated in the same binary culture that I speak about, while the culture you are seeing today in the majority of the world except in Muslim and middle-eastern areas is binary too. The same rules apply to some African tribes still living today in the African continent.

> **Yahukhannan 8:12** Then spoke Yahushua again to them, saying, I am the **LIGHT** of the world: he that follows me shall not walk in darkness, but shall have the light[18] of life.

In fact the above truth is hidden from many and this is the reason why the Jehovah's witnesses peddle their fake white "Jesus" who is only the Son of Elohim and an angel according their false theology. The Muslims peddle the created man Esa. In the Muslim faith he is reduced to man but he at least he is middle-eastern or African origins, which by definition is of the right colour but wrong substance, the Christian "Jesus Christ" who is also white with a rosy looking Slav Blonde actually the image of the illegitimate son of Pope Alexander called Borgia, look at the house of Borgia link below.

http://en.wikipedia.org/wiki/House_of_Borgia

---

[18] Light meaning He is the living Torah. See Ps 119:105, Ps 118:27 and Pro 6:23. He who does not walk in the living which is written Torah does not have life in Messiah because He lives lawlessly.

Are you seeing Borgia in your visions?

The Christian version at least has the correct heavenly attributes but wrong everything else and also in the Christian perverted trinity we have three He's. Unless I am mistaken and I know a man cannot produce offspring from another man. Hint. The Holy Spirit, the Ruach Ha Kadosh is feminine, the Mother and not a masculine "He." See article on the African-Israel website called "Is the Holy Spirit Masculine or Feminine" under Ask the Rabbi.

It should be quite clear to me and many of you, who hold any understanding of the ancient Hebrew and the culture that Sarah our matriarch who was Lot's sister and Lot is an Egyptian name, note Nim-lot an Egyptian name and Nim-rod are similar. Nim-lot was an ancient High Priest in Thebes. Thebes is not the original name of the Egyptian city and is a later derivative.

> **Encyclopedia Britannica**
> The ancient name of Thebes was Wase, or Wo'se. The nome (province) of Wase, the fourth of Upper Egypt, is known to have existed from the 4th dynasty onward. The earliest monuments that have survived at Thebes proper date from the 11th dynasty (2081–1939 BCE), when the local nomarchs (governors) united Egypt under their rule. From this time Thebes frequently served as the royal capital of Egypt and was called Nowe, or Nuwe ("City of Amon"), named for its chief god. The Greek name Thebes (Thebai) may have been derived from Ta-ope, the ancient Egyptian name for ... (100 of 3150 words)

Nim-rod the son of Cush (Ethiopian/Sudanese, Nubian) was related to Abraham's family. These were black African people who traveled from West Africa to the Northern Turkic Hemisphere by conquering nations. This is how both Abraham's father Terach and Nimrod ended up working for each other, clans followed each other. Nimrod's brother Rammah was left ruling in West Africa, which included rule in Eastern Arabia today known as Saudi Arabia. This is how the early Arabs ended up being Black Africans.

Africa had an amazing great culture nothing seen in our modern times, they far surpassed it. The reason why the Caucasians quickly erased black history was due to two reasons one the curses of the Torah for Torah violations that fell on the ancient Y'sra'el the people of colour and two the hatred seen among the white people of today for people of colour whether they be Mexican, Latin American or some other nationals for what we call white supremacy. Yes it does exist in all parts of the corporate and non corporate Caucasian world.

This is not to say it does not exist amongst the blacks but it is a lot more severe in these Caucasian races. When people like Napoleon and his soldiers saw the Sphinx of a black man they could not resist but to shoot it down. Why? Simply white supremacy and racism towards the black race of people trying to demean them. In their foolish narrow thinking they would have thought how could a black man be painted so great. The Egyptian pyramids were made to look like made by Indian looking Egyptians while this is not an accurate picture of ancient Pharaohs at all.

The bright and best men of Y'sra'el were made to look like white ever asked why? Abraham, Isaac, Ishmael, Musa, Yahushua ben Nun, King Dawud, and King Solomon were great black men. King Solomon a man of colour surpassed all the wisdom of Egypt and all other nations put together. This reality has irked so many people that he is no longer painted in his original colour but as a white Caucasian instead. From here one thing is clear Japheth (The third son of Noakh) had and many whites still have an inferiority complex.

Just look at ancient Egypt. Nimrod built a tower that I have not seen even built in modern times to the same height and breath so think about it before you run down ancient cultures. Granted that he built a tower in defiance to Elohim but the modern towers in America are nothing in comparison to what he built and if you think the rich Americans are building towers to give esteem to Elohim, sorry this is simply not true. The Arabs may not have the true Elohim but when they build towers they have their Allah in mind, while Europe and America have become countries where atheism seems to be prospering and Eloah is left in the backseat so to speak.

Even the ubiquitous dollar bill has the symbol of the free masons "All seeing eye" on the pyramid on the back of the dollar bill so what is the point of putting "in God we trust" on it if at the same time you entertain free masonry and occultism? Have we not realized yet that we are destined to fall if we mix worship with idolatry? Then which El? Mammon?

Even the ego today represents similar to Nimrod to say that I can defy you the Creator and build great structures. I know it may be hard to admit our mistakes but realties are very different when viewed from cold facts on the ground. We must look at our self and do some soul searching to see if what we are doing is magnifying Elohim or seeking to exalt our self as great men and women. Even the Brazilian people who built the image of the western white Jesus had the Creator in mind but at least they wanted to represent who they worshipped. In fact this is proof that people of color think very differently. They always have behind their minds how to honor their Creator. So these people would only do what they know best and one cannot blame them for erecting images when they know no better. In ancient Egypt people built big images to their deities and to their heroes.

Ancient Egyptian people were black Africans with the same kind of hair that eventually was also found on the Master Yahushua. Surprised, but you should not be if you were really seeking after the truth. I would not expect to see any different. A man of wooly hair. No he was not Caucasian and he certainly did not come out of the Zagreb Mountains. I expect an African man to look like an African no matter which region he lives in he must carry African traits. One of the things he spoke about is His Father's house. This is an African term in the ancient culture.

The term **My Father's House** was first used in the Torah by Abraham.

> **Beresheeth 24:7** YHWH Elohim of the shamayim (heavens), who took me from MY ABBAH'S HOUSE and from the land of my mishpacha (family), and who spoke to me and swore to me, saying, To your descendants I give this land; He

will send His Angel before you, and you shall take a wife for my son from there.

This clearly shows Abraham whose ancestors were Africans was trying to tell us something. His father Terach was the chief or where all the priests went to meet since he was the High Priest for Nimrod's temple. This is why Abraham used the term to denote what authority his father held. Abraham himself was in line to be the next High Priest but was called out by YHWH to leave his father and to follow YHWH the Master of heaven and earth.

Later the term MY FATHER'S HOUSE was used by other people in the Tanak (Hebrew Bible) and even by Yahushua in the Brit Ha Khadasha (New Testament) writings.

> **Yahukhannan (John) 2:16** And said to them that sold doves, Take these things hence; make not **my Abbah's Beyth** (house) a Beyth (house) of merchandise.

So what does the tem MY FATHER'S HOUSE means in its original context?

This term is clear proof that Abraham and his ancestors were Africans and even Yahushua spoke the same type of language revealing His African ancestry.

In the ancient African culture the idea was of a large hut which was surrounded by smaller huts. You may have spotted this in some modern movies depicting Africans and how they meet.

The chief of the tribe had a large hut where the elders would gather and meet to discuss important community matters. All the huts were centered around this one big hut. Note the two Temples in Jerusalem were in the centre of Y'sra'el. They were the centre of attraction and all of community life in Y'sra'el. The same was true for the Tabernacle. All important contracts exchanged hands in the Temple.

This by the way was an African cultural trait.

```
        ☐    ☐   ☐
   ☐              ☐
 ☐        ┌─────────┐    ☐    Y'sraelite homes
          │Tabernacle│              around it were
 ☐        │         │    ☐         smaller
          └─────────┘    ☐
 ☐
                            ☐
 ☐              ▫
        ☐   ▭   ☐     ☐
```

We'Debar (Num) 24:5 How goodly are your tents, O Yaqub, and your tabernacles,[19] O Y'sra'el.

In the wilderness in the midst of the Y'sraelite dwellings the centre of attraction was the Tent of Meeting with the Ark of the Contract so this was the Father's house i.e. where all the Elders (fathers) gathered to report to the chief of the Universe, our Abbah YHWH and to take important oaths and exchange contracts.

The Muslims took the concept of raising the minaret of the mosque the highest in town which is least understood by westerners.

Behind this the concept is the same yet Muslims do not acknowledge YHWH as their Father but the early Arabs knew the concept which was later applied by the Muslims to their mosques where they lived. In the Muslim culture all important contracts such as life/death and marriages have to take place in the mosque, the structure is the same or a cleric from the Mosque must be present to witness important events.

---

[19] This is a future prophecy which Rabbis know about that means how good are your synagogues/assemblies, places of worship of Israel.

The Bedouins today still apply the same kind of structure around their clans.

One more thing all the African elderly men had to be married and the middle house or hut belonged to the chief. In the Temple the seventy two elders had to be married in order to form a Sanhedrin. The structure in essence was the same.

This structure of a council is still evident in Muslim and African lands where important council decisions are taken by the chief. In Afghanistan this is known as a jirga, you may have heard this word thrown around on TV news probably many times without understanding what it means. In India/Pakistan it is called a punchait where important matters are dealt with related to the local community, rarely any police is involved in such matters.

In these types of councils all the elders would come together and sit down to discuss community matters and then deliberate judgment upon them what was decided collectively. This is where the west gets its idea of a jury in a courtroom. This whole thing is rooted in African culture and before we run down African culture as inferior however most of modern cultures are based upon it while still ignorant of the ancient past.

In the Torah YHWH had a council established of seventy elders plus two (Exodus 24:1) and they would sit to deliberate a matter and enact judgment. There were lower courts and middle courts too. This once again is where in the West we have the idea of lower and middle courts followed by the supreme court.

The structure is the same as the African structure. The question should be asked why? The answer is very simple in that Y'sra'el's people and ancestry had originated from Africa before they were branched out through disobedience to other nations such as Iraq, Iran and further east and west. This is how the Muslims and other nations learned these principles and still live the principles today. Each family has their own brand of elders to decide on important family matters. This still happens even today right in our homes where we are called when we have to answer to important matters in the community.

In the biblical case the term My Father's house is centered upon Yahushua talking about the source of all creation that is the Father and around the Father are His appointed people/elders.

Yahushua a revelation of the Father is the appointed Chief by our Father in heaven (Ps 2:6).

All important contracts were established in the Father's house. We see the Levitical priesthood deliberating on all important matters. Yahushua is also a levitical High Priest and will deliberate on judgment on the nations at the end of time. This should explain what the term MY FATHER'S HOUSE is used frequently in Scriptures. To understand more about who Yahushua was see my book "Beyth Yahushua, the Son of Tzadok, the Son of Dawud.

What about Yahushua calling some of the Pharisees "children of your father, the devil", (John 8:44). How can that be?

> **Yahukhannan (John) 8:44** You are of your Abbah the devil, and the lusts of your Abbah you will do. He was a murderer from the beginning, and stayed not in the truth, because there is no truth in him. When he speaks a lie, he speaks of his own: for he is a liar, and the Abbah of it.

Who were these Pharisees that were talking to Yahushua, were they not part of the chosen nation then why does He call them the children of the devil? Why use such harsh terms? Do these prophesies have meanings beyond the first century or have they all been fulfilled and finished?

One of the questions posed is how can these Yahudim be sons of the devil if they are supposed to be Y'sraelites? The answer is simple. These ones had aligned themselves with the Edomites. Remember Esaw is Edom in Scripture. Though Esaw was the son of Isaac but since he had turned away and went into other false things plus the fact that he was not the chosen prophet but his brother Jacob was to whom he had the inheritance sold.

The Herodians in Yahushua's time were what one can call hybrid Yahudim and they had learnt the Torah while large scale true Yahudim were out of the land. They took over and mixed with the Romans intermarrying with them. The Romans were the sons of Japheth and so Edom and Japheth became mixed seed.

The Herods had become one with Rome and sold out to them. They know that by partly learning Torah they can force obedience but they were not genetic Yahudim. A true Yahudim is one who worships YHWH and follows after him.

While the Edomites, the Pharisees who were arguing with Yahushua were circumcised outwardly, wearing the correct signs tzitzits and tefellin but inwardly they were not living correctly.

Today's Zionists have an idea of a forceful worldly kingdom to be formed in Israel that they could help to bring through the help of the Americans, while today's Zionists think they can do it by money, lying and deception. The Protocols of the Elders of Sion are actually true as they were devised by such types of people and have been in action all these years since their inception, while Christendom defenders of Zionism teach they are a fraud but the truth is otherwise.

The testimony of one Jewish man called Harold Rosenthal confirmed the methods employed were the same mentioned in those protocols. Harold Rosenthal opened his mouth a bit too much and was murdered in a hatched up plot in Turkey to hijack an Israeli air liner in August 12 1976 orchestrated by the Zionists who did not like what he said about their methods. I would suggest the things the said were nothing short of a bombshell and purely by the divine will.

This can be readily searched and found on the net in the Harold Rosenthal Interview with Walter White in 1976 or you can write to me and I will supply you a copy to africanysrael@yahoo.com. A believer had instructed me about the protocols of the Elders of Sion but I never really got around to looking at them until I read the interview supplied by a believer and I then went back and examined the protocols and understood that the Muslims are not lying about the protocols in fact they are telling the truth about them, while Christians none the wiser about such matters trying to defend or discredit the protocols was really another Zionist ploy to avoid people from finding out the truth. In Addition, the protocols were written in early 19th century, while the interview with Rosenthal took place in 1976 conducted by a Christian who had better understanding in the matter. His interview actually confirms all the methods which have been employed to date even in our time it is evident if you examine the corrupt Zionist bankers and media.

Judaism is quite happy to accept that a Jew can be an atheist and a Zionist at the same time, he can be a Marxist and a Zionist but according to Judaism a Jew cannot be a Christian or if he becomes a Christian he is no longer a Jew. This in itself is a contradiction but this is not my worry here. I want to say something about Christianity. In the US the Christian signs and symbols such as Christmas, the cross, the baby and the manger are being removed from Public life and hotly contested today.

I want to point out this is not done by Muslims, they do not have a problem with these in America but this is being done by Zionists. Yes Zionists, they don't have a problem receiving money from Christians and Americans because they know that the Americans and Christians are stupid but they have been trying to destroy Christianity for a while since Zionism or secular political Zionist hate God and his law. I personally know as many of you too know that some of these things are not the true symbols but like it or not Christianity has come to be known by the Cross. I would suggest we do not oppose them in this because at the centre of this controversy is our Master and our Saviour.

Hence why I want to give respect and honour where it is due and what is pagan will be sorted out by Master Yahushua including the cross of Tammuz. The Christians may be wrong in many principle facts or on how to keep Torah but they are not wrong on the death of Yahushua and the fact that He was raised on the 3rd day and He is Almighty God. Many so called Torah followers or spectators are wrong about His deity and running him down as just a man but that is another problem again it hardly concerns me since I both know and have had real life experience with the Saviour as Adon YHWH.

The Christians have and continue to suffer in Islamic nations and have suffered in even the Hindu nation such as India, they have suffered in Buddhist nations such as Burma, Tibet, China and North Korea etc, etc. We must allow them room to learn but should not outright reject Christians but be good teachers to them and help them come to a more fuller understanding of truth. One thing we must not do is support Zionism, which in essence seeks to destroy Christianity and I would not stand for Zionism in anyway shape or form and please do not be confused the root of Zionism is godlessness. If you do not believe me you just need to visit Y'sra'el and see the antics of ZOA, the Zionist Organization of America.

We know in ancient times Rome was into false pagan worship. This is how the Herodians/Edomites became joined to the sons of Japheth and why anyone including the Sadducees (ancient Karaites) who aligned with them would be called the sons of the devil and could no longer be the sons of Abbah YHWH. This is also true today of any person who lines up with socialism, Marxism and any other isms. However if Karaites today want to follow Torah then they are not of this house and must not be treated as such even if they are from Russia as are modern Jews belong to Khazaria and not Y'sra'el.

Yahushua's prophecy speaks at three levels. One of these levels was during his time when some people were trying to fight a holy war and in fighting this war which was not to be they forgot all the rules of Torah, mercy, love and justice even that they were not meant to fight and bring a kingdom with earthly power. The prophecy is applied at a second level to those who today call themselves Jews. The majority of these are converts into ancient Judaism. Notice that ancient Judaism did not function on the Talmud so today's modern Judaism is really Talmudic Judaism. There is a huge difference between ancient Judaism which Yahushua practiced and that which is practiced today. The Shulcan Aruch written by German Jews from Khazaria did not exist (the code of Jewish law) hence many things are foreign to ancient Judaism. The second level of Yahushua's prophecy where he calls them the children of the devil applies during our time and hence forward.

In the late 18th century a misplaced movement arose calling itself Zionism and its goal was to obtain a piece of land either in Uganda which it failed to and then later that became present day Y'sra'el, which they succeeded in acquiring. Their idea was not a Torah centric government but a man-made kingdom which even then they failed to bring about. Even large scale converted Khazari Jews who mainly inhabited Russia and Europe who were supported alongside Christians which today send money to agencies like Exobus and other aliyah (To make immigration to Y'sra'el) types of agencies to take Jews to Y'sra'el is in contravention to the Tanak and the Contracts of YHWH.

All these things have failed and will continue to fail until it is realised who the true progenitors of the Contracts/Agreements are. These were Black people who came in all shades of black from light brown to jet black. You cannot transplant the Hebrew people with Caucasian converts, give them the Talmud and say here you go this is Y'sra'el. Aharon did this when he made the golden calf (Exo 32:4) and said here you go Y'sra'el this is your elohim. This is what is happening today. The Talmud has value to give us understanding but it is not scripture and not holy writ therefore we do not rely on it entirely. We are Hebrews or Hebrew Y'sraelites, we live our faith the best way possible with the information we have. In the ancient time there was no Talmud but there were oral teachings passed down from elder to elder and to the children. The Talmud was a very late attempt to legalise some of these teachings but lots was added to the Talmud in the 6th century CE which were not in the ancient teachings. This is why the Talmud does have the teachings of our elders but we need to carefully sift the information.

Now I want to point out that all those today calling themselves Jews which have lined up with communism, Zionism, Marxism are in the same category and have nothing to do with the children of Abraham or the promise. Yahushua directs his harsh words at these kinds of people today because we cannot strictly apply the words to

Christendom nor to Muslims as neither strictly calls themselves Jews or Yahudi Let's read again.

> **Revelations 2:9** I know your works, and tribulation, and poverty, (but you are rich) and I know the blasphemy of them <u>WHICH SAY</u> they are Yahudim, and are not, but are the synagogue of Shaitan (Satan).

So those who say they are Jews actually commit a blasphemy. Note this is only a blasphemy because they are not Torah keepers.

The synagogue of Satan contains Yahudim (Jews). Which Jews? As I described above however we must be careful not to lump all Jews in this equation and remove the ones who are keeping Torah in order to serve Elohim. I certainly do not count the Sephardic Jews as evil and some of the Ashkenazi but I am very wary of many Ashkenazim rabbis in Y'sra'el teaching hatred of gentiles, these fit in the synagogue of Satan I am afraid as they are doing this by siding with Zionism and trying to have their sympathies and financial support. Rabbi Yosef Ovadia is one prime example of this in Y'sra'el. He said gentiles only exist to serve Jews in the Jerusalem Post paper published in October 2010.

http://www.jpost.com/JewishWorld/JewishNews/Article.aspx?id=191782

Christians and others who have a misplaced love for Y'sra'el are really into idolatry because our command was not to worship Y'sra'el but to worship it's maker. Today Christendom and those who are into Torah quickly run up with if you increase Y'sra'el then you will be increased. This is not entirely true. Would YHWH benefit us if we benefit atheism, Marxism and gayism? No. This is what today's allegedly chosen people Y'sra'el is into and famous for, gay annual marches in Y'sra'el These people in Y'sra'el are Zionists and not chosen, they created themselves yet they belong to Russia, Europe and other parts of the world while the real chosen people black in colour sit in exile in Europe, America, and in the east waiting to be restored back to the land promised to Abraham another Negro.

In order to benefit Y'sra'el we must first learn who is genetic Y'sra'el. These poor forsaken Y'sraelites are stuck in Africa, India, Pakistan, China, America and Europe so how could you say benedictions for transplanted self aggrandized converted Russian Jews who have no genetic link to Abraham? So those who run to the land and raise up just these Jews are into idolatry. See my book World War III, the Second Exodus, True Y'sra"el's return journey home to learn some real hard facts of the Bible and future prophesies yet to be fulfilled.

If Yahushua is YHWH then who should we hold higher? Your love should be for YHWH who is revealed in Yahushua. Your love should be for His Torah and His commandments. We are to be with our husband as we are the allegorical wife of Abbah YHWH. Our husband is not right now in Y'sra'el (the physical land) he is in exile with us so don't go running off to Y'sra'el selling all your possessions to face mortal danger because that is what will be. The <u>synagogue of Satan</u> was not just said by Melek Yahushua in isolation where the majority Jewish European/Russian converted people stand as they are not obeying the Torah.

I also say once again this precludes those Yahudim who keep the Torah and are strictly not going to the land to stay there such as the Iranian and other Jews in the West who according to the Torah standards classify as right-ruling even if they may not be genetic. They know what I have just said. It is forbidden to go to the land to permanently stay there until the Messiah returns. Their love is correct and not misplaced while Christians today would be better off to support the black Jews in Ethiopia and in Africa and Asia. That is where the true ancient Yahudim are to be found and sorry not in Y'sra'el but many in America yes. If you ask me Y'sra'el has only ten percent real blood line genetic Jews and the rest 90% are gentiles and it does not matter if they wear skull caps and hold Torah scrolls or not.

In Y'sra'el you will find Russians and Europeans who call themselves Jewish but they are more likely to have the blood of Attila the Hun and Changez Khan then ancient Y'sra'el. Get your bearings straightened out and sort out your love and do not just ignore the words of Yahushua who called them the **synagogue of Satan** in Rev 2:9. Satan has the counterfeit synagogue this is where institutions like the IMF, the World Bank and others fit. Did you know the American Federal Reserve is controlled and owned by the synagogue of Satan. Why do you think the dollar bill has the "Egyptian pyramid symbol" on it? Coincidence, I don't think so.

If we love our Master then we pay attention to His words. We must not allow ourselves to be aligned with Zionists, Marxists ideologies that are the frame work of the One World order and illuminaties. We need to wake up. Today's wars are not fought for helping the poor Afghanistanis and Iraqis or let's go and help the Libyan civilians. When you follow the trail it leads to the synagogue of Satan. Let us serve Yahushua our Master and heed his words. Either we are the children of the devil or the children of the Most High. Either we belong to the Synagogue of Satan or Synagogue of YHWH. Choose Life.

We know that the sons of Japheth took over the land of Y'sra'el and dwell in the land and fully pretend to be the sons of Shem.

The Prophecy of Noakh said it would happen in Genesis 9:27 and that prophecy has been fulfilled. This prophecy states that the sons of Japheth will go to dwell in the homes of Shem and so much so that they will call themselves Shem. This is true today. Noakh by the way was an African born to an African father but he was not black but born an albino (white) never the less he had the African traits. His ark also landed in Africa so don't go running off to Turkey to look for it. See Article here, "Noakh's Ark where did it?" land.

http://www.african-israel.com/Ask-the-Rabbi.html

Therefore Elohim will do a restoration in the future for the true sons of Shem those called the twelve tribes. Today Y'sra'el may as well be empty and the restoration in 1948 was man's effort and not Elohim's unless you believe that your and my pittance $100 is going to restore his people. YHWH never asked for it so don't do it to give money to send people to go back to the land when its clear that is forbidden but no one will tell you this except me here. Your money will give you more increases if you had invested it to someone in Ethiopia, Sudan, Ghana, Nigeria or even for the true Y'sra'elites in Pakistan and India as there are people there who are the true Children of Y'sra'el and many sons of king Solomon wait in Ethiopia in utter poverty. Next time you look, I suggest you look to these nations. We must help our brethren in exile where they are.

Yahushua challenged the Pharisees from the school of Shammai and the following conversation took place with them:

> **Yahukhannan 8:19** Then said they to him, Where is your Abbah? Yahushua answered, You neither know me, nor my Abbah: if you had known me, you should have known my Abbah also.

He tells you they do not know His true Father in heaven. This must have come hard to these Edomites and they must have snarled at Yahushua that he is saying they do not belong to YHWH. Well if you do not belong to the El our Father then you can only belong to one other being and that is Satan and his camp. This is clearly saying you do not belong in our camp and the only other camp is the opposition party. Be warned brethren and stop appeasing people who are not the true Y'sraelites. Support people who are true and spread the bibles such as the Hidden-Truths Hebraic Scrolls by the boxes, the message of our Master Yahushua.

I want to remind you what Yahushua commanded us:

> **Mattityahu 28:19-20 19** Go therefore, and make disciples of all nations Utvilotym Atem B'shem shali (Immersing them in My Name). **שלי בשם אתם וטבלתם 20** Teaching them to Guard and Do ALL that I have commanded you: and, lo, I am with you always, even to the end of the age.

How do you go to all the nations? By leaving the land!!!! So what happens if you don't go? You are a disobedient soul.

Did Yahushua say give money and take people back to Y'sra'el from the nations? No. There is no mandate for us to do so. This is not our job but when this happens it will be directly by the hand of Yud, Heh, Wah, Heh (YHWH). We must not think we are in His place. We must not fall into misplaced love and idolatry. Our mission it to go and teach Torah to the scattered Y'sraelites who will be found right amongst where you live. Go to your poor neighbourhoods you will find them there.

You won't find them in the millionaire streets. In the cross Atlantic slave trade millions of blacks who belonged to the House of Yahudah were taken into the USA and Europe. It is those we must reach out to in love. It does not matter today if you are Black or white but it does matter if you love Yahushua and obey His Torah that makes you a fully counted Y'sraelite you go and reach His people. May that be with food, clothing and of course the true gospel which is Torah and proclaim the King came 2000 years ago and will be returning soon and should find us in the midst of His people helping, teaching, reaching out to broken hearted people.

You can play a tremendous role. Are you ready? You can join us as we are sending the HTHS Torah's to many American prisoners and other places. All those who ask will get a free FREE Torah in the prison system as they get to know us and we get to know them. All they need do is ask and we will give it FREE. There are probably Mexicans, Latinos and others around you who are from scattered Y'sra'el. Even if they were gentiles our mandate is to go to them with the Torah and teach them. This is the Benefited work Yahushua wanted us to do while we wait for him. Did he say build me a Temple? Then why are you?

Did he not send His disciples out of the Land of Y'sra'el? Then why are you selling everything to go back where he told you to leave from? Don't fall in with unwise people and end up ruining what has been given you. Look and examine carefully, He tells His disciples not just the twelve it includes you and me. Was Thomas stupid to go to India? Did you know he went through Africa to India, why? Because many scattered Y'sraelites were in Africa back then and are still today. Was Peter foolish to go straightway to Iraq? If you allow the synagogue of Satan (misplaced Zionism) to colour your thoughts then only Elohim can help you because you are already lost.

Our love is not misplaced but in the right place. We are to be a light to the gentiles. How will you be a light if you go and hide in a corner in the middle-east and then fight the Arabs all the time? The Arabs have been denied the gospel by the Zionists and including foolish and unwise Christians who side with Zionism because of this misplaced agenda have isolated them. They have been denied access because they only see aggression from the so called Jews (converted khazars) the synagogue of Satan. How will they ever come to know the Master if Zionism stands between them? Zionism will fall!!! Yes Zionism will fall and all those that support it will fall with it.

The truth will spread because we the true servants all together will join hands and reach out to the Arabs in love and with materials to reveal the truth while the Zionist domination will utterly fail.

It is a curse for disobeying the oaths not to go to the land of Y'sra'el permanently to live and try to take it by force. The Zionists and all who support Zionism are today laughing at Elohim but Elohim will have the last laugh. Don't fall into the curses. Jus this year a British woman was killed by the name of Mary Jean Gardner, she may well have been alive today had her leadership known better.

Another British woman last year was almost killed who did Aliyah.

http://www.guardian.co.uk/world/2010/dec/19/israeli-briton-stabbed-american-killed

Kaye Wilson, a British citizen who moved to Israel in the early 1990s, was found on Saturday night with her hands tied behind her back, bleeding from several knife wounds. Will people listen to what we are trying to teach them, its not yet time to go back to the land please don't be blinded by others around you who know no better. Choose life.

I have been honest with you and told you so be ready and prepared. May Yahushua our Master help you all to see the truth and in turn use you wherever you are.

One of the key questions I ask people who claim to have seen our Master is what colour was He, please describe His hair colour, what type and description of his body features? It may seem like a foolish question but it is meant to weed out the chaff. To date I have not found a single person who has described his facial makeup or hair type correctly which is why I can very quickly reject the western white "Jesus" that many keep seeing in their dreams and visions. Too much TV and Roman Catholicism.

These people get very upset at the white 'Jesus' they have seen or perhaps describing another different one altogether.

Usually after this they find the nearest exit to leave.

To date I have only found one woman who described Satan to me with absolute clarity and perfectly correctly, she is British and saw him on the edge of She'ol/Hell and was indeed correct in her description. Satan is Jet black also with a princely forehead and he can change himself in various ways. She saw him become like a bulldog and that scared the living daylights out of her but she knew that she had seen the real deal. She also saw the Master but could not describe him as was not privy to His face or body because she just saw light surrounding a person from a distance on the edge of She'ol (paradise). Once again her description was accurate but there were other things of her vision/dream which told me she was telling the truth.

The Master increase her for her testimony. Another British woman a famous Muslim convert on the other hand who has claimed that she saw the twelve disciples descended in her room is a false embellished testimony and totally unreliable so we need to be careful not to run off after visions which may not be what we think they are. Some visions are reliable and must come to pass while others are not.

My ex-wife saw a vision which came to pass in exact details step by step to the behest of my personal pain when I would have wished it was not true. I do not challenge all visions but only those that are false. The reason for that incident in my life was YHWH showing me and doing some soul correcting for me in some distant past mistakes I did with my Muslim ex-wife when I would not listen to her and be angry with her for no good reason (I had apologized for my behavior to my ex-Muslim wife first before I had gone before YHWH) and it was also to teach me the importance of marriage to see my own marriage fall apart and the pain of divorce which I felt every minute to teach me the ills of divorce and the pain that children go through with further illustration on how the Most High felt when He divorced his northern bride (The House of Y'sra'el). Today we all quite happily think let's get divorced and move on. It's not that simple. I told the Master don't put me through the pain because I am only human and not in His shoes and He is vastly more patient and merciful then I ever can be.

He showed me a glimpse of how it feels to lose someone you love so much and even today I feel the pain in my bones when I think about it.

Keturah

Abraham's wife Keturah lived in the South and was likely his first wife followed by Sarah as his second wife and then the third wife Mashek followed by the fourth Hagar who was the daughter of the Pharaoh of Egypt which was given to Abraham as a gift when he came out of Egypt (Genesis 12:20). That is when Abraham had made a pact with Pharaoh. The text clearly tells you she was an Egyptian in Genesis 16:1, which tells us where she came from and she was not just an ordinary woman but the daughter of Pharaoh an important princess while most of you have just made her a mistress of Abraham and almost de-legitimized her. All the ancient Pharaoh's were black and so was she which means Y'shma'el was Black in complexion too. Ancient Y'sra'el was an African country now read between the lines.

The text of Yashar 12:59 (The book of Jasher) tells us that Eli'ezer was a gift to Abraham but if you thought that he came wrapped in a package with a ribbon attached to it then this will be a mistake. It was Eli'ezer's mother Mashek that was a gift to Abraham as a wife in the Northern Alliance but she then gave birth to Eli'ezer as Abraham's concubine/wife. Mashek was from Damascus which explains that Nimrod ruled this area in order to give a woman here as a gift to Abraham. (Note I told you earlier they were related)

According to Yashar 13:5 Abraham was fifty years old when YHWH came to him to ask him to leave the land with his wife and household. This indicates to us that at fifty Abraham was already married but notice that in Yashar 12:59 Eli'ezer is a grown up young man which illustrates that Abraham was already married to Keturah from which the gift of the maid his third wife came to him because she was connected to Keturah's family side and Keturah was already living in Canaan/Y'sra'el so Abraham was familiar with the land of Y'sra'el as a child because his father often went to visit the land to meet his wife (Abraham's mother) there and Abraham would have visited the land before also as a baby. When I first came to faith I was told the bad teachings that Abraham never visited the land but later on examining scriptures by the Spirit of YHWH (The mother Ruach Ha Kadosh) prompted me to re-look in Genesis to see and understand that Abraham was very familiar with the land he was sent to. Ancient Y'sra'el was a nation with lots of little kingdoms. It was not a single nation like the USA today or the UK with one central government. If you look at 15th century Africa then Y'sra'el was like that. In Africa existed at least fifty to a hundred kingdoms with local chiefs, princess and kings. This was like Y'sra'el. We read about it in Joshua 5:1, 2:1, 7:2. Yericho was one kingdom and Ai another.

Abraham was from the priestly Horoite clan and it is historically known that the Horoites lived in Bethlehem in ancient times. The Horoites believed in Horus as the son of eloah and that he will one day come as the son of god as a man and wear the two crowns.

Abraham's mothers was in Beersheba who would have controlled water wells and his father controlled the water resources in the North of the river Euphrates and its tributaries as the king's (Nimrod) general and High Priest in his army. He maintained Nimrod's temple of idols and Abraham was the next in line had he followed his father's false religion (Josh 24:14).

Who was the first born son Isaac or Ishmael? Actually neither, Yoktan (Yokshan) is the firstborn of Keturah she lived in Beersheba and Abraham was already married to Keturah before he acquired Hagar as his fourth wife, she was an Egyptian princess (Gen 16:1).

Keturah likely to be the first wife named her son in her great grandfather Joktan's (Gen 10:25) name which was the common custom and is shown with others too in the Torah such as Isaac and Jacob. Abraham had two wives followed by Mashek the third wife given to him by Keturah through Nimrod and Sarah giving him Hagar an Egyptian princess which totals four wives. Sarai is not the name of a woman but a black tribe and one that exists in Africa so this reveals Abraham's black ancestors. Sarai (my princess) her real name was Y'skah, in ancient Hebrew Y'skah means "Beautiful bright creature."

The ancient Yud was the picture of an eye 👁 hence why the term bright. Sarah/Y'skah was a beautiful light brown skinned woman. If I compared her to a modern black woman then Halle Berry would be it though I would go one further and say she was even more prettier than Halle Berry.

Though the moon does not have any of its own light but reflects the sun's light so this is not a description of her colour as of the moon but just her beauty since the ancient Samech is the picture of the moon. ☽. Remember I spoke in part 1 about ancient Hebrew like Egyptian was originally a monosyllable language. The first character is what mattered but the additional characters gave meaning or shape to the first character. In order to know meaning of the character the first character is what did it. Now that sets up all the scholarship on its head that claims that Hebrew is made of two letter roots. Not true.

Sarah was Abraham's half sister (Sister wife) and Keturah was his cousin wife from Mother's side Matrilineal. We find the pattern in the Tanak of people of noble birth or princes having at least two wives one from the father's side and one usually from the mother's side. This was common practice in African/Asian cultures and is even today. Note all three women Sarah, Hagar and Keturah were black women and the ancestors of the African people while the Gnostic literature written much after the gospels depicts them as white which is falsified Greek text. Keturah would be taking care of the family inheritance home of Abraham in the south while Sarah would have been taking care of the inheritance home in the north in Shechem. Keturah's six sons eventually ruled the whole of the Arabian Peninsula. The Rabbis incorrectly teach people that Keturah and Hagar are the same. This is a false Zionist teaching beware. They spoon feed these kinds of erroneous teachings to church seminaries who then spew out the same error under the auspices of the Zionist rabbis.

Abraham was a prince and chief (Gen 23:6). Such type of people always had at least two wives with lineages from both parents while they often also took extra wives to protect the property and extend the sons to regions under their control. Hagar was of Egyptian descent which was part of the North African region

Isaac had two wives, Jacob had four wives, so it's clear our people lived in a patriarchal model. Just because you did not know it nor understood it does it matter to YHWH who created the laws?

> **At the council of Toledo, in A.D. 400, it was ordered, by canon seventeenth, that every Christian that had both a wife and a concubine should be excommunicated; but he should not be excommunicated who had only a concubine without a wife. At the fourth council of Carthage, A.D. 401, it was ordered, by canon seventieth, that all bishops, priests, and deacons, who had wives, must repudiate them, and live in celibacy, under penalty of deposition from office. Pope Innocent I., about A.D. 412, in his official letter to the two bishops of Abruzzo, orders them to depose those priests who had been guilty of the crime of having children since their ordination. Thus the seeds of**

Gnostic error, that had been sown in the church during the former periods of its history, now sprang up anew, and bore a plentiful harvest.

Are we going to allow monastic, ascetic, anti-Semitic church fathers to define our Torah based faith that existed from four thousand millennia ago that was even practiced by our forefathers such as Abraham, Isaac, Jacob, Moses and King David amongst some heroes of our faith? These people are listed as the heroes of the faith all over Scripture. I would side with Torah and be "Free" any day then to live by the views espoused by ascetics, who had no clue that God's first order was "**BE FRUITFUL AND MULTIPLY**". Personally I would tell them go take a hike. Now if someone wants to be fruitful with one wife which is highly unlikely they may try but the only way one can be fruitful is with plural wives at least two just as Abraham had four wives and he placed his wives in the North and the South axis for the greatest eternal benefit. Both wives became the progenitors, one of the Hebrews, and the other of the Arab race.

Chapter 5
Kosher or Unkosher

By using Paulos's letters which are not sacred and not halakik (agreed by Torah standards of living) it was made to look like that Y'sra'elites no longer eat kosher and can consume any kind of meat or food. Let us look at some examples of how the clergy twisted Sha'ul's and the disciple's writings.

> **Mark 7:17-19** After he had left the crowd and entered the house, his disciples asked him about this parable. 18"Are you so dull?" he asked. "Don't you see that nothing that enters a man from the outside can make him 'unclean'? (19) For it doesn't go into his heart but into his stomach, and then out of his body." (In saying this, Jesus declared all foods "clean.")
>
> **Mark 7:17-19** (HTHS) And when he had left the crowd and entered the Beyth (house), his disciples asked him concerning the parable. **18** And he said to them, are you also without understanding? Do you not understand, that whatever thing from outside enters into the man, it cannot defile him; **19** Because it enters not into his heart, but into the stomach, and goes out into the intestines, purging all food.

    He is showing that generally acceptable kosher food according to Torah enters the mouth and leaves via the normal digestion cycle. He is not saying reject all of the Torah and now go and eat unclean foods like pigs and crabs. Unfortunately those unlearned in the nations have done exactly that under the guise of favor. The words added in the KJV translation (In saying this, Jesus declared all foods "clean.") are a scribal addition and not in the manuscript.

  The context is very important and here most people take this verse completely out of context as the issue at hand is about **washing of hands** that we can read in Mark chapter 7:1-3 where the Pharisees and the scribes had a tradition to wash their hands before eating of food but since the disciples were not following it in the similar fashion though they were washing their hands but differently, while the school of Shammai's Pharisaic formula was somewhat more different and was not followed by the disciples as they adhered to the school of Hillel's formula. You can see this described in verse three "holding the tradition of the elders".

In Addition, many people do not realize that the words **"in saying this, Yahushua declared all foods clean"**, actually do **not** exist in the text but are inserted by **anti-Torah/anti-nomian** Christian scribes for good measure to mislead others. Why would Torah obedient Yahudim even be discussing the eating of swine? This is not the context and no need for such arguments when they are already fully understood.

> **Mark 7:1-3** Then Pharisees, and certain of the scribes came together to him, which came from Yerushalim. 2 And when they saw some of his disciples eat lechem (bread) with defiled, that is to say, with unwashed, hands, they found fault. 3 For the Pharisees, and all the Yahudim (Hebrew people), except they ritually wash their hands first, eat not, holding the tradition of the elders.

Why would you want to argue this verse out when it is not even talking about the kosher laws?

> **Acts 10:15** And a voice spoke to him again the second time, "What YHWH has cleansed you must not call common."

The Yahudim saw the gentiles as unclean people and why wouldn't they since the gentiles were involved in all sorts of pagan idolatry, eating of unclean foods worship to false gods thus the Yahudim who wanted to live a pious life and be respectful to YHWH's holy laws and remember they had to attend the Temple and they could not attend the Temple being in a state of ceremonial uncleanness because by the touching of unclean foods would render the person ceremonially unclean until evening (Leviticus 22:6) and if a person had eaten unclean food then touching that person would render you unclean also.

Here YHWH gives instruction to Kefa (Peter) not to call gentile people unclean so the issue was never about eating unclean meats but about gentiles being unclean or not. YHWH wanted the gospel message to be taken to the gentiles so He showed Kefa that he could go to the centurion's house and meet with him. Remember the Yahudim did not even want to enter a gentile home for fear of becoming unclean. One of the other reasons was that gentiles sometimes buried their dead loved ones in their homes also.

Likewise is the problem of an observant Muslim who does think around similar lines. Hence why many Christians living unclean lives have been unsuccessful to reach Muslims and Yahudim.

> **Romans 14:1-3** Now receive the *Y'sra'elite* brother who is weak in the belief, and do not have disputes over differing opinions. **2** For one believes that he may eat all things: another, who is weak, eats only vegetables. **3** Let not him that eats despise him that eats not; and let not him who eats not judge him that eats: for Elohim has received him.

Paulos is not advocating eating unclean foods but shows us that Hebrew believers generally had problems eating with the new gentile converts. In the Hebrew halacha it was established that first of all you do not eat with the gentiles but if you do eat then it is safer to eat vegetables since they would not be sure if the meat is clean or unclean from the gentile homes and also if cut right or not cut right and many other factors. Traditionally it is forbidden to eat from a gentile.

Paulos is saying is that, if a Hebrew decides to eat with a gentile, judge him not, let each individual decide however this is quite wrong to do so. This is why we can see the Acts 15:29 injunction was important about food as it's a big stumbling block, when eating with the people of the nations, who do not do things according to Torah principles.

The issue here was not clean versus unclean but vegetarianism versus meats that were acceptable. Some people had decided to go vegetarian considering it was very difficult to tell if meat that was acceptable i.e. sheep/goat from the market was offered to the idols first or not, rather than take risk they wanted to avoid it altogether.

> **Colossians 2:16** Let no man therefore <u>judge you in meat</u>, or in drink, or in respect of an holy day, or of the new moon, or of the Sabbath days.

The issue here was simply that in the first century Judaism Pharisees were fasting at least one day to two days a week to look right that is on Monday's and Thursday's and so they were saying that if you do not fast then you cannot be right-ruling.

Paulos would not be judging YHWH's holy Sabbaths as there was no question about these. In fact the word for "man" is not just any man but pagans who would judge you for meat or drink and so Paulos admonishes to not worry what the gentiles, think of what the believers are doing i.e. keeping the Sabbath holy, obeying and observing the new moon and eating Kashrut. The judgment is only in the house of YHWH and not outside. The term 'man' is rabbinic for ha Adahm meaning the goyim or the returning ten tribes.

> **First Timothy 4:4** For every creature of YHWH is good, and nothing to be refused, if it be received with thanksgiving."

Christians jump to the conclusion that we can eat anything. The absurdity of this argument is that we should accept dog, cat and snake equally with thanksgiving but this is not what was being said so YHWH does not leave us in the dark, the answer in fact lies in the next verse.

> **1 Timothy 4:5** For it is **sanctified** by the **word of YHWH** and prayer.

Which foods did YHWH <u>sanctify</u> to be taken with thanksgiving? You can find the acceptable ones in Leviticus 11 and Deuteronomy 14 these are the ones that are <u>sanctified</u> or set-apart. Christians want to believe that YHWH is holy, He will not allow sin in His sight but He would not mind His followers relishing in things He forbids, right? How wrong are such notions?

> **First Timothy 4:3** Forbidding to marry, *and commanding* to abstain from meats [broma], which YHWH hath created to be received with thanksgiving of them which believe and know the truth.

Ask yourself today who is asking to refrain from these things? Meats that are to be taken with **thanksgiving** e.g. Hindus don't eat beef yet YHWH has allowed beef as good meat. There are many other religions which want you to remain vegetarian or drop meats from your diet that YHWH did not forbid yet this all flies in the face of what our Creator wanted and really it is distorting YHWH's holy laws by deceiving individual people. However the Greek word "broma" here could well mean food which is to be eaten and not necessary for animal meats. If you give up something so it does not offend another person then that is your choice but not a commandment.

> **1 Corinthian 10:25** (KJV) Eat whatever is sold in the meat market, asking no questions for conscience' sake;

> **First Qorint'yah 10:25** (HTHS) Whatever is sold in the market places, which you want to eat, scrutinize, judge and be sure asking questions for conscience sake:

One can clearly see the KJV translation is incorrect in its translation. We must ask questions before we eat so that we do not break YHWH's Torah in ignorance that is what the Greek text says not what the churches have been ignorantly teaching. We can see when you use Paulos's letters one can easily be led astray.

We need to ask questions. The Strong's word used here is G350 anakreno means to scrutinize, to judge a matter rightly. The word is not in the negative but in the positive that means ask if not sure.

We must remember that the concern or context of this verse is not unclean meat versus clean but common acceptable meats sacrificed to idols versus those that are not sacrificed to idols stated in 'First Corinthians 10:18.' Furthermore, most Christians who perhaps did not look into the early 1st century culture did not grasp this verse will for sure jump to the conclusion automatically that this is regarding meat when it regards something greater. Remember the Hebrew people would never need to have a debate on food whether the kosher laws are for them anymore or not as these are clearly explained in Leviticus 11, so why argue over established doctrine? Have you ever seen Muslims argue over food? They take many laws out of the Torah too and never argue over them.

Would you sit in with a Chinese and eat snakes fried without asking questions? I have been to China on a number of occasions and I always ask questions about which food is right or wrong for me in a restaurant. Do you think I am just going to go and eat snails, crabs, lobsters and even fried scorpions which I have seen commonly sold in the shopping malls?

The context of First Corinthians 10 is not a discussion whether the Hebrew diet is right or wrong but the context is adultery and idolatry mixing seed so the context is not breaking Torah but how to walk right. Paulos starts with a discourse on Y'sra'el and its ways then coming out up to verse 14 says do not do likewise else we would likely face the same results in other words Christians cannot escape judgment for living idolatrous lives. Paulos is using proof texts by admonishing the people from Deuteronomy 32-16-17. Many similar discussions took place amongst the Hebrew people. In the Talmud we have a similar discussion in Chullin 95a as follows: 'If there were nine meat shops, all of them selling ritually slaughtered meat and one shop selling carrion, and a man bought meat from one of them but he does not know from which of them he bought, it is forbidden because of doubt.'

> **1 Corinthian 10:27 (KJV)** If any of them that believe not bid you *to a feast*, and ye be disposed to go; **whatsoever is set before you, eat, asking no question for conscience sake**.

The KJV translation is greatly at fault. Here is the corrected translation in the Hidden-Truths Hebraic Scrolls Bible.

> **First Qorint'yah 10:27** If any unbeliever invites ye, and ye be disposed to go; whatever is set before you, scrutinize, judge before eating asking questions for conscience sake.

We need to ask questions and that is the correct context! The Strong's word used here is G350 anakreno means to scrutinize and to judge carefully, the other Greek word supplied is Strong's G3357 meden which also suggests to pass, depart, go as the case maybe.

Now let's do some testing and if a host presents you with a fried chopped up snake and you are not sure so what will you do? Are you going to eat it with thanksgiving asking no question and just in expectation that YHWH will make it beneficial even what is unclean and no amount of benediction will turn it into a clean kosher creature? How about a skewed rat, what if it is a human being, are you still going to eat it and give thanks? Or have we forgotten that people in different parts of the world do eat these things, so where do we stop? We must learn to be trustworthy and believe and trust YHWH that is what belief is about and His Torah Leviticus 11 was given not for Him but for our guideline to stop us from second guessing our food habits.

In First Corinthians 10:27 it is easy to understand that in context it refers to knowing what is right from wrong. Many believers would do well to learn from the Hebrew people. The Hebrew people are right the black plague was one such incident blamed on The Yahudim in Europe, when many Europeans became ill and blamed the Yahudim because the Yahudim did not acquire the diseases due to the clean Torah food laws they were practicing. The reality is that The Yahudim trustworthily kept the food laws to this day. Therefore, they avoided many illnesses proving that following YHWH's laws have many benefits. Queen Elizabeth I moved her court to Windsor castle to avoid the disease and made it lawful to hang Londoners coming her way. This is how serious it was at that time. Today the swine flu with over a hundred thousand cases in a short space of time does the same killing without prejudice both young and old and we wonder why.

Paulos was not an apostle and at best just a witness which is the what the word in Act 14:14 means. Beware he is the false apostle described in Rev 2:2. His entire message contradicted that of the Messiah but this book is not about Paulos and another one is in the pipeline to be released next year called Paul of Tarsus the Thirteenth Apostle.

The Fat is YHWH's

> **Leviticus 3:4** `the two kidneys and the fat that is on them by the flanks, and the fatty lobe attached to the liver above the kidneys, he shall remove;

3450 years ago YHWH instructed Moses that they were not to consume fat. Did YHWH know that fat is bad for us? Well the one who created us knows what is good and what is bad for us better than we do, today we talk about high cholesterol levels yet YHWH knew these things and revealed for us to avoid them. Marvelous or what, great.

> **Leviticus 3:17** This shall be a perpetual statute throughout your generations in all your dwellings: you shall eat neither fat nor blood.' "

Where ever the word **perpetual** is used it is the usually the word Ha' Olam. It means the commandments were made with the twelve tribes of Israel and so should be kept with all later generations.

The Yahudim do not argue like Christians do today about obsolete or not obsolete but faithfully obey YHWH in these matters. The Muslims are very similar in that they also stick to the laws enshrined in the Qur'an but why wouldn't they since they are both cousins and act similarly but poor Christendom argues over everything and make an issue over nothing, why not just believe YHWH and leave the rest to Him to decide. Remember Abraham believed YHWH and was credited **with right-ruling**, here is GRACE for those spiritually blind to see this in Christendom.

Are you willing to believe YHWH or argue endlessly?

If this writing has made you realize your error then repent and obey YHWH our saviour. On the other hand if you think that you know better than the author writing this and you want to continue to live in sin and ignorance then you are leading to your own destruction and are responsible for it.

It's simple you start with kosher food bought from the Jewish stores and if you do not have Jewish stores then the Muslims stores are your next best bet to buy meat which has been drained of blood. It's not true that Muslims sacrifice the meat to idols. Muslims say Bismallah on the sacrifice and Allah hu akbar.

Allah the deity of Islam is not an idol in the Ka'ba today as in ancient times and Muslims sincerely believe that this is the name of the unseen God. The term Bismallah is taken from B'Shem YHWH which the Hebrews recited meaning "In the name of YHWH" and Muslims simply applied it to their god Allah so it comes directly from the Hebrews and the Hebrew language.

If you are going to apply the meat commandment then to be consistent you need to apply it to everything else. That means also you should not work with them or do business with them and you will soon find that the interpretation of Acts **21:25-27** is actually misplaced by Christians and even Jews who use it the so called converts to Christianity.

Elah is the Arabic word for God. Just because they say Bismallah on the meat it does not make it unholy. Choose for yourself what is right.

Question) Do Muslim put a statute up? No. then how can you even conclude that they worship idols? Just because they do not know the one true God it does not mean they worship an idol. A Hindu worships an idol and you can find many statues such as Vishnu, Krishna, and the Hindu god Ganesh. This would mean we are actually forbidden from eating from Hindus. Then what would you do if you had to buy live animals from them? The answer is that you would buy the live animals and slaughter according to Torah.

> **First Corinthians 8:10** For if someone weak see you who possess knowledge dining in **AN IDOL'S TEMPLE**, shall not the conscience of him which is weak be strengthened to eat those things which are offered to idols;

Look where the people sat and ate. In the temple of idols.

The food sacrificed to idols must have their priesthood present just as our priesthood was present to sacrifice to YHWH in the Temple. Have you seen this with the Muslim butchers or slaughter houses? No chance of that ever happening because I have been to these places.

The Muslims priests are not present in the slaughter house so once again a negative and to tell you they do not have a statue or idol parked so to speak in the Mosque or butcher's place. We cannot look at the spiritual and lump it on to the Muslims who have no such knowledge.

So unless you can prove that both of my negative statements can be made positive in light of the Torah the case fails and you can eat meat slaughtered by their hands as it is done by slaughtering the animal cutting the jugular veins bleeding it to the ground this is actually what Torah requires.

Memondies one of the greatest respected Yahudi scholars stated the following in the egeret ayman the epistle to the Yemenite Jews when asked by them if the Muslims worship idols and are pagans. He stated no they are not pagans and are not idolaters, they do not know paganism because it has been purged from them. He also stated that if you enter a land and the only place you can find there is a Muslim mosque then you are allowed to go and do your prayers there and if you enter a land with no mosque and no synagogue but only a Christian church then do not enter the church your prayers are forbidden. What does this tell you?

Chapter 6
Circumcision for all males

If we say circumcision is for all males then the next question is what about Galatians and what Paulos wrote there in?

> **Galut'yah 5:6** For in Yahushua The Messiah neither brit-milah (circumcision) avails anything, nor uncircumcision; but faith which works by love.

First of all I want to be absolutely clear if no one has had the courage to say this before that Sha'ul known as Paulos can write whatever he likes, his letters are not halakhic, which means they hold no binding authority for us. Our authority comes from the law, the Torah of Moses. If you use Paulos's letters to break the Torah then you are in severe violation of it and will be judged for it. Paulos won't be saving you nor standing in place of your judgment so think carefully what you are doing. Circumcision is not conditional but unconditional contract with Abraham and is not annulled. Paulos was not a true apostle but is not the discussion of this book and another book will be written devoted to that subject of his alleged apostleship.

In order to decipher this letter and this particular chapter a few things need to be understood. First, Paulos commonly known as Paulos was a Pharisee in the first century, the title of Rabbi and Pharisee is usually synonymous at least for our purpose of study. A Rabbi in the first century would not teach to disobey God's law because everything a person did in the first century would be judged by the laws in the Torah, by the Jerusalem Sanhedrin. Anyone who did not obey the law of God would be seen as an evildoer and this is why many Romans at least for the Jews in Israel fell in the camp of evildoers, gentiles and dogs because this was the designation given to gentiles.

They were considered unclean, filthy and outside the Contracts and ways of God. This letter is not written to a Church called Galatians or place name even but the Hebrew word Galut means dispersion so this letter is written to the dispersed ones and these were understood in Rabbinic Judaism as the Ten Northern tribes of Israel who were understood to be settled in Asia Minor which is today's Turkey. This is at least what Paulos thought albeit incorrectly.

This letters composition is considered to be from around 46 CE to 54 CE depending on various theories of north and south of Galatia however I would like to add that the letter is to the dispersion of the Ten lost tribes of Israel which Paulos saw as coming back home to the faith through Messiah Yahushua who has repaired the breech. If Paulos was found to be preaching against the law of God that would land him in serious trouble with the Temple authorities and the Jerusalem council who would want to maintain control in the dispersion and the function of the synagogues was to link back to the Temple in Jerusalem. Note because of various accusations he did land in trouble with the Jerusalem Beyth Din (House of Judgment) and hence we see the council in Acts 15 issuing various directives for gentiles joining Israel or for returning back to the Olive tree (Israel).

We need to understand Paulos was not in a modern church setting but in a synagogue setting. Israel did not make churches but made synagogues, while most are quite happy to know that Paulos was writing to some church out in the north this is not the case. Once you start changing words and start to apply your 21st century surrounding it is then that everything starts becoming blurred and you start to lose the real issues at hand.

What is also not understood is that Paulos was trying to correct these messianic synagogues to conform to the required halacha (way of living) according to his understanding though albeit unfortunately not always correct and against the principle faith. Unfortunately thanks to Paulos's errant teachings modern Christianity has already concluded that the law/Torah of God has been abrogated and they are now a law unto themselves, while the law of God states that it is everlasting and irrevocable.

> **First Chronicles 16:17** And has confirmed the same to Yaqub for a law, and to Y'sra'el for an everlasting Contract/Agreement,

Contracts/Agreements can only be everlasting if the law remains but many Christians lack this understanding. For them the law is abrogated but then how can a Contracts/Agreements be everlasting? Christianity needs to resolve this problem that they have created for themselves, the problem with most Christian denominations is that they pick and choose what suits them and most of them walk contrary to God and His ways. By walking contrary to God and not obeying His commandments, and also serving other gods in such things as Easter, Lent, Christmas and other Christian unclean days, which are festivals of false gods foreign to YHWH and at the same time saying I have peace is a self created deception.

> **Debarim (Deut) 29:19** And if it comes to pass, when he hears the words of this curse, that he speaks benefit for himself in his heart, saying, I shall have shalom, though I keep my halacha (commandments) with a rebellious heart,[20] the watered ground with the parched:[21]

Many today that walk in such things will neither have the Benefits of Elohim in their life nor the peace that comes with the shed blood of our Master Yahushua since they are still committing sins and have put under their feet, the sacrifice committed on the Mount of Olives by the Master Yahushua. They will also forfeit the 1000 years of reign by their actions that is yet to come as they will lose their first resurrection.

How could King David proclaim keeping the law/Torah <u>forever</u> and ever if it was going to be abrogated later at the death of the Messiah? Note, King David will be raised in the millennium and will be keeping the law of God. Indeed

---

[20] This is the categorical state of most in Christianity. The majority of them walk in utter rebellion and trying to **Increase** self while sticking to the pagan ways of their forefathers popularly known as the church fathers. Our task in life is not to behave like this and **Increase** self, because when we are walking Torah then YHWH will **Increase** us and not self.

[21] Idiomatic expression to mean whatever this person touches will be cursed that includes friendships and business and he will bring judgment on whole nations if he be a king or leader.

King David was right that He and others like him will be obeying and guarding the law forever and ever.

See our study called "Will Christians be raised in the thousand years reign in the millennium period" in the African-israel website.

www.african-israel.com/Ask-the-Rabbi.html

> **Psalm 119:44** So shall I keep your Torah/law continually forever and ever.

So the premise is always going to be that the Torah/law of God is eternal and this is the basis Paulos is working from.

> **Galut'yah 6:15** Neither brit-milah (circumcision) is anything, nor uncircumcision, but the only thing that matters is a new creation.

A lot of Christian Pastors read from this letter of Paulos not to circumcise and are quite wrong if that is the knowledge they have come to.

Now for them Paulos even outweighs the greatest leader and teacher of the Torah Moses called out by YHWH. Does Paulos say in his letters you shall not circumcise? He kind of reads it this way that circumcision does not have value by which most latch onto not doing circumcision any more. This is why Paulos here and in some others places confused the people.

No Contract/Agreement can be annulled while the circumcision is a Contract/Agreement sign. I have to also let you know that Paulos' letters cannot be used to formulate new teachings, he has no authority from God irrespective if you think he does as he does not have two witnesses saying as such.

Let's look again.

> **Galut'yah 5:6** For in Yahushua The Messiah neither brit-milah (circumcision) avails anything, nor uncircumcision; but <u>faith</u> which works by <u>love</u>.

Paulos does a kal v' chomer, which is light and heavy using the seven rules of Hillel.

Paulos is not negating circumcision or saying that uncircumcised men are better than circumcised men but simply reducing everything down to the common denominator, of 'love'. Those who circumcise but do not know how to love YHWH and their fellow man have fallen from grace and those that 'love,' meaning keeping the commandments of YHWH. The Torah drives us to love YHWH and His creation. He echoes the same words in First Corinthians 7:19. Note Yahushua also said this in John 14:15. The problem is the way Paulos said it was quite wrong and confusing and hence led to people stopped following the everlasting contract to circumcise so in this regards Paulos's words are wrong the way he conveyed them.

The Hebrew word for love is אהב which kabbalistically reveals something quite deep to us. It consists of the three Hebrew letters of Alef, Heh and Bet. I explain these in my book Hebrew wisdom, Kabbalah in the Brit ha Chadasha.

Alef is the source of all the universe and is related to our Father in heaven from whom we also receive the Ruach Ha Kadosh (Em Chockmah, mother wisdom the Holy Spirit) and the Son Yahushua. They are in these three letters. The Heh is significant and reveals the Ruach Ha Kadosh, while the Beth reveals the very first beth used in the Torah in Genesis 1:1 for the word Beresheeth. This signifies the House of our Father in heaven on which He set His Son Yahushua as King (Ps 2:6) to rule and reign. The word Ahav equals the numeric value of eight in Hebrew Gamatria, which also reveals new beginnings and connects us to the celebration of Tabernacles when the Son Yahushua was born and reveals the Shemini Atzeret the 8th day which will start at the completion of the Millennium reign for those obedient to Him.

Note also that before even God gave circumcision the Egyptians were circumcising both male and female in their priesthood. It was unthinkable for an Egyptian priest to marry a priestess who was not circumcised. The black Egyptians narrowed it down to those not circumcising being unclean and filthy and not fit for marriage. Hence why we see Yosef's marriage with a priestess who would have been circumcised and so was he when he married the daughter of Potipherah the Priestess of On Gen 41:45. We see Elohim take it a level further by making it into a Contract/Agreement/Contract/Agreement to be part of His priesthood so that all males in Y'sra'el circumcise.

> **Galut'yah 5:15** Neither brit-milah (circumcision) is anything, nor uncircumcision, but the only thing that matters is a new creation.

It is true that those who merely circumcise only to follow a ritual after some man's law system are not followers of YHWH's true Torah and those who do not circumcise also follow after a law designed by men such as in Christendom are both deniers of the true Torah of Moses and neither is better than the other. The Muslims who circumcise but do not follow the Torah are a good example of that alongside Christians who do not circumcise.

The laws established by the school of Hillel are binding on all believers as Yahushua agreed and followed all of them. So those that tell you that the Talmud is satanic or Mishnah is no good are people without knowledge and understanding and should really be avoided. I would not waste my time even debating such characters unless I want to debate them on TV or publicly.

> **Genesis 17:14** And the <u>uncircumcised</u> male child, who is not circumcised in the flesh of his foreskin, that person shall be **cut off** from his people; he has broken My Contract/Agreement.

Elohim has the ability to cut off people who refused to obey Him and if you keep refusing after your rescue you will be counted as a rebel and not allowed to enter in the kingdom.

We are citizens in the kingdom of YHWH and I am a Lewite who is to live my life serving Him in the exile in accordance with his Torah. The day I refuse to obey I have to seriously consider death as the end of my life. So all of you out there who want to follow the wicked path of unbelievers please spare me your reasoning and keep your do not circumcise benefits to yourself. Do not try to dictate or violate what God has said to do in favour of your fickle imaginations. God will always be right and you will always be wrong for discarding his commandments.

> **Act 15:1-2** And certain men which came down from Yahudah taught the brothers, and said, **Except you be circumcised according to the custom of Musa** (Moses), **you cannot be saved**. 2 When therefore Paulos and Bar'nabah had no small dissension and disputation with them, they determined that Paulos and Bar'nabah, and certain other of them, should go up to Yerushalim to the apostles and elders about this question.

The Custom of Moses,' was a shorthand idiom for doing the circumcision according to the oral Torah to make you a full Ger-Tzadik (see footnote Acts 10:22 in the HTHS Bible) before you could call yourself a full proselyte in Judaism and this particular group of the Pharisees obviously adhered to the full and immediate Ger-Tzadik formula, they did not believe in going the minimum, which was called Ger-Toshav, which would mean keeping the seven Noachide laws established by the Rabbis for converts.

These would not be doing circumcision and immersion until a year later after having understood the seven annual feasts. It is probable that these people were saved no doubt but were not at the point of circumcision and Baptism according to the Ger-Tzadik formula hence the reason why this dissension arose. They would have wanted to see a process of Ger-Toshav by passed to full Ger-Tzadik before the believing Pharisees would agree that these are the community of Israel.

Those people who will be alive and try to enter the Temple but have not been circumcised at the return of Messiah will not be allowed to enter the Temple and refused entry until they go and get circumcised and then they will have several restrictions too lengthy to explain here.

> **Ezek 44:9** Thus says Master YHWH; No foreigner, uncircumcised in heart, and uncircumcised in flesh, shall enter into my sanctuary, of any foreigner that is among the children of Y'srs'el (Israel).

Brit milah, physical circumcision is not an option but mandatory as it is one of the **SEALS OF THE FAITH** and the Contract/Agreement given to father Abraham which was **Everlasting**, which means FOREVER. Those people who are not circumcised including Christians will not be allowed in the Temple and there will be no magical circumcisions for them. Also those that teach you not to do it are simply messy Messianics devoid of Torah and customs of our fathers.

Circumcision is an eternal Contract/Agreement and must be done for males on the 8th day of their birth.

> **Genesis 17:10** This is My Contract/Agreement which you shall keep, between Me and you and your descendants after you; every male child among you shall be circumcised.

If you claim to be part of the Abrahamic Contract but do not adhere to the requirements of the Contract, which is circumcision then you have nothing whatsoever to do with Abraham. It does not matter how many times you quote Paulos his apostleship is self proclaimed, it's both irrelevant and as I said his letters are not halakhik. Paulos was not a true apostle as many teach as Yahushua spoke directly against him in Revelations 2:2. Their were other false apostles beside him in Turkey.

Now with this understanding in mind we can tackle chapter 5 of Galatians and start to understand each individual point behind the words without glossing over the text.

> **Galatians 5:1** (KJV) Stand fast therefore in the **liberty** by which Christ has made us free, and do not be entangled again with a yoke of bondage.

Now the reason I explained a little about the Passover is because at that time Israel was in bondage or bondage to the bondwoman (Egypt) and slavery to the world as Egypt was a type of the world and its human laws.

Galut'yah 5:1 Stand fast therefore in the liberty wherewith Messiah has made us free, and be not subject again with the yoke of slavery.

We have already examined the word liberty but let us examine it here a little more at the spiritual level.

The Greek word for liberty is Strong's G1657 el-yoo-ther-ee'-ah, which can basically mean "freedom."

Let us look at the Hebrew word under the hood and see if this connects anywhere spiritually and allows us more insight to the term. The two Hebrew words we will look at are Strong's H1865 "Daror," which is used for the Jubilee and actually takes us back to the year of the Jubilee, when all the captives were set free and the Hebrew word Strong's H7342 "Rakhov," which means broad, large, wide, and for direction. If we now take the last letter of Daror, which is the Hebrew letter ר resh and the last letter of Rakhov, which is the Hebrew ב beth we end up with the Hebrew word Rab or Rav which means GREAT, MASTER, Prince, Mighty amongst a few terms רב. All terms which apply to our Master Adon Yahushua. This on a spiritual plain connects us back to Yahushua the God of Israel revealed in the flesh THE GREAT Rabbi of Israel the greater Moses and the greater Solomon.

Unfortunately such writings of Paulos did confuse many and therefore cannot be used to defend him or make him into some kind of an apostle.

Now let us identify the yoke of slavery. Whenever Paulos addresses these cryptic terms one can be sure he is referencing the Torah of Moses versus the world's law/torah or yoke of slavery which many have taken upon themselves the so called humanists of this world. Let's examine the wording in the book of Leviticus.

Jeremiah 2:20 (NKJV) "For of old I have **broken your yoke** and burst your bonds; and you said, `I will not transgress,' when on every high hill and under every green tree you lay down, playing the harlot.

God had broken the yoke of Israel of "slavery" but they still committed sins against God. The yoke was the slavery of the world rather than submission to God, which was required in order to remain free in the House of the Master.

When Israel was in bondage they were in the **yoke of slavery** so God brought them out and then declared the following.

> **Lev 26:13** (KJV) I am the LORD your God, which brought you forth out of the land of Egypt, that ye should not be their bondmen; and I have broken the **bands of your yoke**, and made you go upright.

The term that is used in the book of Leviticus is 'Bands of your Yoke" or Staves or fetters of your slavery. God is iterating our responsibility towards his instructions, the law of God through Messiah who is the person who came to re-teach us the Torah that we are responsible creatures and for us to stand tall we must stand in His rule of law and avoid man's law and it's pitfalls. The Hebrew words vaolaych etkhem kom' meyoot means "**made you walk straight or upright** as it is used in Leviticus 26:13.

A slave was not free to walk straight or upright but a freed man was able to walk straight. Since the Messiah has done the tikkun olam (repairing of the breech) of the worlds therefore we can walk erect and straight but there is a responsibility on our parts to uphold God's instruction known as the Pentateuch or Torah. As long as we possess and walk with God's law in our hands we cannot be slave to the devil but when we reject the law of God we are no longer walking in freedom.

The Hebrew term Kom 'meyoot the word that means we are emancipated and can now stand tall, this is only used once in the Tanak (Old Testament) and we need to be careful not to be confused with Paulos' letters else instead of freedom we could be in bondage as many others under the wrong authority. This indicates that there is responsibility attached to our freedom and it's not just to roam around and do whatever we like kind of ideology that is and has been preached in places of worship.

We are given choices which need to be made wisely. The other Hebrew words for freedom are "Yahroot" and "Akhravoot," which also means responsibility for our lives. In all honesty there can be no genuine freedom if we do not have rules to show us how we are to live in our day to day lives. God gave us these instructions and we have to decide wisely how to be part of His kingdom community.

After throwing away our "**yoke of slavery**" as Paulos tells us we now have two choices according to Hebrew tradition in which Paulos was brought up and he accepted them all and never rejected them contrary to popular opinion. The ones mentioned in the Hebrew tradition are Ol Malchut Shamayim (The Yoke of the Heavenly Kingdom) and Ol Malchut Ha Mitzvoths (The Yoke of the commandments). We must take these upon ourselves.

Our rejection of these and God's Contractual terms will put us under the **curse of the Torah** in which the law of God tells us this fact in Leviticus 26:36.

> **Lev 26:15, 36** And if you shall despise my statutes,[22] or if your soul abhor my judgments, so that you will not do all my commandments, but that you break my Contract/Agreement: (36) And upon them that are left alive of you I will send faintness into their hearts in the lands of their enemies; and the sound of a shaken leaf shall chase them; and they shall flee, as fleeing from a sword; and they shall fall when none pursues.[23]

The Hebrew phrase **Kol aleh nidaf aleh radaf** meaning "**the sound of a shaken leaf shall chase them**." This means when we reject the law of God and we are living outside of Israel in the Galut (dispersion) so take note that this applies in all ages not just those in Turkey in the past that then we shall hear a leaf fall and feel really frightened because we have rejected the God of Israel and his kingdom rule. This is happening to many Christian

---

[22] Many even today despise the Torah as a Hebrew thing, and still refuse to do the commandments written in the Torah. Such as the eternal loving annual feasts YHWH gave us, so that our children will learn the truth and not go astray.
[23] Always fearful of your enemies roundabout

communities in Pakistan, India, Africa because they have ignorantly rejected the rule of God because of bad leaders.

The sages of the Mishnah and Talmud said the following "**kabalat ol malkhut shamayim**," the receiving of the Yoke of the Heavenly Kingdom is not about "I will take it on when I feel comfortable and remove it when I do not feel comfortable." Likewise today many in Christendom have chosen easy options and to live in worldly ways rejecting and abrogating the law of God and putting themselves in the captivity.

Paulos should have made it clear that he was taking us back to the Shema Israel creed in (Deut 6:4) by this for more look up See Berachot 13a in order for us to understand our responsibility.

The yoke that the Messiah offered was the same yoke of the Kingdom. Many only do lip service to Yahushua while rejecting His yoke in ignorance of church traditions that were totally anti-Jewish and anti-Bible.

> **Matt 11:29** Take my yoke upon ye, and learn of me; for I am meek and lowly in heart: and you shall find rest to your souls.

Yahushua directs us back to the scripture verse in Jeremiah 6:16, which is back to Torah. These are the ancient paths to find our rest, which is rescue through the Messiah, who clothes us with His right-ruling. The next statement is what Judaism teaches and we agree:

> The Yoke of Torah, Rebbe Nechonia ben HaQanah said:
> --"He who takes the yoke of Torah on himself shall have lifted from him the yoke of kingdom and the yoke of the world's way. But he who takes the yoke of Torah off himself shall find laid on himself the yoke of kingship and the yoke of the world's way." --- Mishna, Aboth 3.5

Remember the leaf analogy above, you can only find Shalom, the complete rest, rescue, freedom, security, peace even during times of conflict if you take His yoke His Torah hand delivered to Moses. Rejecting is it rejecting life.

Ask yourself today have you done this and if not then why not? Is you life in peace and if not then could this be your central problem?

Have you rejected the 7th day Sabbath because your church said no to it or you read from Paulos's writings regarding Colossians 2:16? Have you rejected other principle laws of hygiene and food such as what is clean to eat and what is unclean such as pork and shellfish? Paulos actually drives home some deep points but I doubt many out there have understood even half of his message and instead arrogantly use his writings to abrogate the law of God. How can this be?

Have you rejected other principle laws of hygiene and food such as what is clean to eat and what is unclean such as pork, shellfish and Crabs? If you are using Paulos's writings arrogantly to abrogate the laws of God. How can this be?

> **Galatians 5:2** (KJV) Indeed I, Paulos, say to you that if you become circumcised, Christ will profit you nothing.

As we continue to read with understanding that we must uphold the law, the rule of law delivered by Moses and rubber stamped by Yahushua/Jesus of Nazareth then is Paulos now telling us that we should not circumcise and if we do circumcise then we will have no benefit? This is how many old and modern churches in the world have read this verse and decided to use Paulos as judge and jury to reject the law of God!!! What a travesty? If they did that then they have fallen into what I described earlier in the "yoke of slavery." So what is Paulos a circumcised Jew telling us? Is he telling us that what is good for the goose is not good for the gander? If it was good for Paulos who was himself circumcised then how can he now teach against it? Yet Paulos himself declares in Galatians 5:11 that it is good to be circumcised which means he did at times teach circumcision and other times did not hence why he ended up confusing everybody. It appears to me he was a confused man. He was not an apostle and he was not appointed by the Master Yahushua since the

Master spoke about three false apostles one being Paul in Rev 2:2.

The Church severed itself from Israel and put all the Jews down as unsaved and repressive. There were many groups of Judaisms in the first century assemblies but there was no church. Indeed there were various synagogues and the believers went to the synagogues where the Orthodox Yahudim taught Torah, while most of the believers were Yahudim and had no problem proclaiming the law of God and even circumcising physically.

Paulos' problem was not with circumcision removing of the foreskin but with using circumcision as a tool to say that you are saved and only a member of God's club if you circumcise in a certain way according to some of the Pharisees. The term had come to be known as hatafat dam brit (drawing of a drop of blood) and peri'ah (removing the membrane) meant a lot more than just removal of a bit of skin. You would have had to do this with each new group that you joined as they rejected the circumcision that you had received previously and then you would have to obey all their rules else you could not be a member of their club the same as today's denominations each with its own rules. This is where Paulos went wrong and did not explain to people why he did this. His confusion led many astray and caused many to reject the Torah of YHWH. He also gave a flaky testimony in the Book of Acts which does not tally with his experience being different when you check the book of Acts

However when Paulos objected to this theology of the first century where a certain group of Yahudim demanded that new converts coming in must circumcise in this particular fashion and then obey their legal rulings (Note the problem was not with the way of circumcising the flesh and is still done this way by a mohel, a Rabbi expert in the art of circumcision). Some men who had come down from Jerusalem and had said unless this is done with immediate effect we will not proclaim that these gentile converts have been saved and are a part of the community of God. In other words they would still see them as gentiles and outside the body of Israel. That would have caused a lot of problems as they would not be welcomed in many synagogues of the land. The brothers from Judea were not wrong since they understood what it meant to incorporate gentiles in and if the gentiles were not serious they would cause a lot of contention.

> **Acts 15:1** (KJV) And certain men which came down from Judaea taught the brethren, and said, **Except ye be circumcised** after the manner of Moses, ye cannot be saved.

The manner of Moses, was a shorthand idiom for doing circumcision according to the oral Torah to make you a full Ger-Tzadik (see footnote Acts 10:22 in the HTHS Bible) before you could call yourself a full proselyte in Judaism and this particular group of the Pharisees obviously adhered to the full and immediate Ger-Tzadik status, they did not believe in going the minimum first, which was called Ger-Toshav (God fearer), which would mean keeping the seven Noachide laws established by the Rabbis for converts for at least one year before you become Ger-Tzadik.

The procedure of Ger-Toshav would not require immediate circumcision until a year later after having understood the seven annual feasts and other terms in the Torah of Moses which was being taught in synagogues on the weekly Sabbaths. To Paulos at least these people were still redeemed and part of the community no doubt but were not at the point of circumcision and immersion according to the Ger-Tzadik formula could wait hence the reason why this dissension arose. The Pharisees that came up from Judea wanted to see the process of Ger-Toshav bypassed entirely to full Ger-Tzadik for these gentile converts before the believing Pharisees would agree that these would now be part of the community of Israel. I personally see Paulos as wrong to argue with elders about agreed ways of doing things which worsened the conflict.

Christendom use this text not to circumcise proving Paulos to be a false apostle. Circumcision can never be done away as it's part of the contract given to Y'sra'el.

It was accepted by Paulos that circumcision was/is an eternal commandment in the Torah but this group from

Jerusalem said they wanted things to progress very quickly before the new converts completed the Ger-Toshav formula. Paulos knew this would be problematic according to his personal opinion as the halacha (Way of living) set by some teachers and he wanted the new converts to wait, understand and then circumcise using the 1st century Ger-Toshav (God fearer) formula, which would still make them part of the community of believers and therefore the physical act of circumcision would come later.

Paulos used the argument that since circumcision was given to Abraham after he was saved this means no man needs circumcision to be saved but by faith. But faith or contracts came out of the Torah and for you to proclaim something out of the Torah you would have to acknowledge those contracts and hence this was problematic because you cannot claim salvation with lip service, an act had to be done.

A lot of people are still confused about this and think that the Torah saved the Yahudim by works of the flesh but the reality is that it never has stated this explicitly because salvation in the Torah was always by faith through obedience, acceptance, and execution of those contracts/agreements. Some even think that the Torah was saving people by some sacrifice in the Tabernacle but once again this is incorrectly taught in many churches because there was **no** sacrifice for intentional sin and never has been. If there has never been a sacrifice for intentional sin then how could any Yahudi ever be saved by a sacrifice or human work? Ask your Pastor to explain this one.

Intentional and unintentional sin

Many people think that there was a particular offering for intentional sin but the Torah does not prescribe an individual offering for intentional sin. You might ask what about the feast of Yom Kippur. This offering would cover for the corporate guilt of the whole community of Israel yearly both intentional and unintentional sins but there was only one problem with it like any other sacrifice that it was not automatically accepted. For Israel to know if this was accepted or not they would have to tie a scarlet string to the horns of the altar and then wait and see if that turned white. If that did not turn white they knew that God had rejected the sin offering. In other words our rescue was always by grace and never by works. The tying of a string has nothing to do with a Torah ordinance but the Hebrew people took this for atonement from Isaiah 1:18 and the inference in it.

It is recorded in the Mishnah that the scarlet did not turn white for a whole forty years after Yahushua's death and resurrection. Why would it since Yahushua was the sacrificial lamb once and for all times. This string did not turn white but that does not mean YHWH has decided to now change His laws or that He rejected His contracted people. What this means is that the Messiah the one door of Israel was now to cover the whole 12 tribes of Israel including present day and future day Judah who were obeying Torah in the dispersion. The Yahudim were from that time forward to remain in spiritual blindness until the return of the Messiah but this does not mean as many Christians think that the Yahudim are no longer saved and are going to the lake of sulphur. Please see our series of Salvation of the Jews on youtube.

http://www.youtube.com/watch?v=YyiZ5QhfhEo

Pastors usually take this out of context by denying the Torah of Moses and telling people that you do not have to be circumcised. This is not true, Paulos is not saying do not get circumcised but circumcision had come to mean different things in the 1st century which could be to obey some of the branches of the Pharisees and Saducean established laws such as takanot (fences), gezerot (prohibitions), minhagim (Various customs established by the rulers in the Temple) etc. Some of these stated gentile people to be circumcised immediately, without any understanding of the Torah and to start to follow all the customs and commandments of the elders so in affect a person was circumcising for the wrong reasons and this would indeed be a problematic.

Paulos here tells people in affect do not circumcise but fails to explain do not do it for the wrong reasons, first the heart needed to be circumcised as stated in Deuteronomy 10:16, and then after the believers acquired understanding, they could circumcise and become a Ger-

Tzadik, a right-ruling convert. That is what Paulos should have explained clearly but since he did not it was left loose and many people were left in confusion.

If we look at Romans 5:1 Paulos argues to be made right-ruling by faith alone and not by works of men and this is not something new that Paulos came up with because this was always the case before the Messiah came.

> **Galatians 5:4** (KJV) You have become estranged from Christ, you who attempt to be justified by law; you have fallen from grace.

Is Paulos saying that you do not need to be circumcised now because if you do then you are estranged from the Messiah? Many take this passage apply it this way believing exactly this and then refuse to circumcise males. This is because they have not understood the full grasp of the passage.

The King James Version is not very accurate here at telling us what law Paulos is talking about however here is a more accurate translation from the Hidden-Truths Hebraic Scrolls.

> **Galut'yah 5:4** (HTHS) Messiah is become of no effect to you, whosoever of you is <u>justified by the human law</u>; you are fallen from favour.

You are better to get the Hidden-Truths Hebraic Scrolls from the www.african-israel.com website to get a better understanding of scriptures or you will continue to fumble in the darkness with misapplication of scriptures due to incorrect translations. I am telling you categorically there is no better translation out there and you can quote me on it. No person has spent the time to teach people that I have and no person has put back what was removed this is guaranteed but this project is on going and will be until I am removed from this earth this can be sure and I will continue to teach the people of the Messiah Yahushua what is the truth so that our lost people can be restored fully to His Contracts.

Here is what one Pastor wrote after reading the first edition which has now moved on to the 4th edition which is even more accurate. Please note we changed the name from the AF Bible to the Hidden-Truths Hebraic Scrolls.

> Having obtained some 6 months ago, a copy of Rabbi Simon Altaf's translation of the Holy Scriptures, "AF Complete Bible", I have engaged myself in an intensive study of his work, diligently comparing its translation with many other translations, both old and new.
>
> Being a deeply devout student of the Holy Scriptures for almost 45 years, and having read and studied a vast amount of varied translations in my ministry as Pastor, Bible-teacher and Evangelist, I confess that I am amazed at the depth of understanding, knowledge and revelation that Rabbi Altaf has concerning the sacred text.
>
> One is immediately struck by the vast amount of scholarship, study and devotion to the text that has been put into this work. That this is a work of par excellence is beyond doubt.
>
> Rabbi Altaf's intimate and seemingly endless knowledge and understanding of the Aramaic and Paleo Hebrew languages have well qualified him to undertake such an awesome and responsible burden as this.
>
> The translator takes his readers on, not only an intensive, but also an exciting, exhilarating and exuberant roller-coaster ride of eye-opening vistas of Elohim's word that undoubtedly have not been researched, expounded on, nor explained for centuries.
>
> Not only does he clearly explain and reveal the need of Yahuweh's people to know and utter the sacred name of their Elohim, but he shows the necessity of full-Torah observance, 2 house theology and the doctrine of the Ruach ha Kodesh among many other hitherto hidden-away truths.
>
> Not only is this translation so unlike all others in that it dispels with the Greek-mindset that has

blinded the eyes of many a serious Bible-Student in previous translations, but it restores fully the true Hebraic understanding which has been either lost or (deliberately) hidden for the best part of 2.000 years, for as the serious student studies this work, he may well be startled with the statements made in the thousands of footnotes provided in this work, but Rabbi Simon Altaf isn't bringing out a `new revelation`, no, rather he strips away, layer by layer, almost 2.000 years of a Greek mind-set which has dominated the Hebraic text, to reveal at long last, the lost and hidden Hebraic understanding which ancient Hebrew sages and prophets knew and walked in.

I humbly and heartily endorse the study of this translation by every truly-seriously-minded student whose desire is to get to the very roots of the Aramaic/Hebraic understanding of the sacred scriptures and to walk in its truth.

Finally, it is absolutely evident that this work could not have been undertaken without the help and guidance of the Ruach ha Kodesh who leads us into all truth. To the one true Elohim who has revealed himself as Abba Yahuweh in creation, the Ben, Yahushua in redemption and Ruach ha Kodesh in sanctification, to him be glory, le-olam va-ed; Amein. **Pastor Denis G Beedie (England, UK April 18th 2010) www.torahtreasuretrove.com**

When we look at the life of the patriarchs, we are shown in the Torah that Abraham was justified by faith alone in Gen 15:16, while circumcision was indeed given as a Contract/Agreement in Genesis 17:10 later. This is when Abraham received and became circumcised who was already saved by faith alone and then he took his son Yshma'el and circumcised him at thirteen and also circumcised his male servants including Isaac upon his birth. Therefore circumcision is indeed a very important contractual command to be done after we are saved and certainly not to be ignored.

Those of your who have used the letters of Paulos and decided not to circumcise your sons or yourself if you are male then you have put yourself under the curse of the Torah that Paulos himself spoke about in Gal 3:10.

Biblically rules specify that each doctrine is validated by two witnesses therefore even if you interpreted this letter this way that is just one witness now where is your second witness? You will not find Matthew, Mark, Luke or John ever saying any such things therefore this puts you and anyone else on a very dangerous ground because now you are under the curse until you start to obey the Torah. The curse is not removed by the blood of the Messiah because the blood of Messiah is for the removal of sin tied to the Contract/Agreement in Deuteronomy 29 and certainly not for the removal of curses as incorrectly believed.

> **Deut 27:26** Cursed be he that does not continue in all the words of this Torah to do them.[24] And all the people shall say, Amen.
>
> **Gen 17:13** He who is born in your Beyth (house), and he who is bought with your money, must be circumcised; and My Contract/Agreement shall be in your flesh for an everlasting Contract/Agreement:

If you claim to be purchased and redeemed by the **blood of the Messiah** then you are **brought for a price** but if you refuse to circumcise still then you are a gentile and a **heathen and nothing to do with Abraham and his household**. This is indeed clear in the Contract/Agreement.

Note, the Contract/Agreement is part of his household and anyone refusing to do this is not part of his household, it's very simple.

---

[24] Anyone even claiming to be a believer who does not continue in all the words is still under a curse even if he claims to be in Messiah. The Messiah only removed the curse of transgression and the second death. There are many curses written in the Torah and there are also many favorable Increases, in order to reap these you have to 'hear and do,' the words of this Torah. These curses are separate from the Messiah of Y'sra'el, which people usually mix up with Increases and curses.

The spirituality behind circumcision. To remove the femaleness behind a man. When a person does not circumcise it is understood that he carries the traits of both male and female at birth and thus it is <u>circumcision</u> that allows the side of maleness to dominate the person. Without doing this the male is confused, have you noticed how many homosexuals we have in our society who are uncircumcised?

The primary reason is that when we circumcise we shed the blood which is an absolute requirement for any Contract/Agreement. Without the shedding of blood there is no remission of sins Heb 9:22.

If we refuse to shed blood of our little skin which is useless anyway if left on and can cause various diseases later because dirt and dust entraps there then it only goes to show that we are not willing to meet Elohim on the part of the Contract/Agreement that He requires us to do so hence therefore there is only one conclusion that those who do not do it have no part of the Abrahamic Contract/Agreement because it is not a verbal but a physical.

Some questions;
Question) What if I just came to faith and am uncircumcised, when shall I do it?

Answer) You can wait up to one year and learn the faith but then you must do it only if you are a male. Find a doctor who can do it for you then you can do a hatafat dam brit drawing of blood yourself. if you are in England I can advise on which doctor to go to. There are registered mohel's (recognised circumcisers) in the USA too.

Question) I am a believer but I did not know that I should circumcise myself or my son but I want to do it since I just realised I was taught wrong so now so what do I do?

Answer) Find a Jewish doctor and get your son circumcised as soon as possible, there are directory listings both in the US and UK for these folks. You can usually Google this.

Question) Can I celebrate the feast of Passover without being circumcised.

Answer) You can join in the feast to learn its principles but you cannot partake of the meal until you are physically circumcised (Exodus 12:44). It's a sin for you to take part in the meal until you are properly circumcised.

Chapter 7
A look at Ezekiel 37 again

Y'sra'el's resurrection

Many Christians who read Ezekiel 37 love to allegorize it to mean something that it does not mean by saying it's about us being born again. Or they say it's about Ysrael who will one day join with us when they hear of Jesus but Jesus is not even the real name of the Messiah but His name is Yahushua. Notice I did not use the term "was" His name because He is alive and ruling from heaven. How can he be the same today if He is not alive?

Let me ask a question if Christians are right then the following should be true.

> **Ezek 37:12** Therefore prophesy and say to them, Thus says the Master YHWH; Behold, O my people, I will open your graves, and cause you to come up out of your graves, and bring you into the land of Y'sra'el.

If this has the Christian born again interpretation then did YHWH raise Christians from the dead in their graves in their countries and place them in Ysrael? No, this means the Christian interpretation is at best flawed and laced with inaccuracies. Are we surprised?

Did we see a second Exodus anytime after Yahushua's resurrection yet? So that is a problem with modern interpreters they run ahead of themselves while they continue to get themselves wrong.

The other interpretation by both Jews and Christians on this is that this is speaking about the return of Jews back to the land in 1948 and that God is restoring them back! Really that is news to me since I never heard about this twenty years ago which means it's another falsely applied prophecy. When the second Exodus event occurs it will be so big and so magnified that the whole world will know something is happening in Ysrael but since I did not know it and many others knew not then we can safely rule this out as the event is yet future for real Israelites and not lawless Christians. Rebellion is not rewarded with an entrance to the physical kingdom on earth but rebellion is kept out of the camp and dealt outside the camp or did you know this. Those Christians that do not keep the Sabbath and do not apply the other laws of circumcision, kashrut, etc are living in danger but are happy to live ignorantly so let them be and go to their own demise.

> **Ezek 37:14** And shall put my Ruach (Spirit) in you, and you shall live, and I shall place you in your own land: then shall you know that I YHWH have spoken it, and performed it, says YHWH.

If YHWH took the Jews to Ysrael in 1948 then did He put His spirit into them and did He establish a Torah government? Are not those people filled with the Spirit of Elohim supposed to create a Torah government? If the answer is No, which is obvious then this is indicative that this was not the gathering by YHWH's hands.

So this cannot apply to 1948 which has been falsely applied by uneducated people in our scrolls given to the Hebrews. Just because one can read the bible from cover to cover it does not mean that person can understand it too.

Then who does the prophecy really apply to? This applies to true Ysrael which is still outside Ysrael. Did you know that people who live in Israel are still counted in Exile? This should be telling that if they are still in Exile then how could the restoration have taken place?

> **Ezek 37:25** And they shall dwell in the land that I have given to Yaqub my servant, wherein your ahvot (fathers) have dwelt; and they shall dwell therein, even they, and their children, and their children's children forever: and my servant Dawud shall be their prince forever.

If the Jews as well as the Christians falsely claim that the Jews have been returned to the land and the prophesies have been fulfilled or partially fulfilled then where is Melek Dawud in their midst? He is supposed to be raised and put back in Ysrael as a leader upon them but I don't see him, do you? Where is he hiding? I see nothing of his likeness in government. Something is very wrong with this picture in present day Ysrael. King Dawud who is a black king is not there and the majority of the Israelites that he is supposed to govern are AWOL (absent without leave).

Who are these people who call themselves Jews in Ysrael? Are they the real Semitic people that inhabited the land in 1450 BCE?

It's like some Hollywood blockbuster where a King is dying and orders his missing son to return to claim his land and inheritance. In the meantime the king dies but he leaves instructions about which country his son is likely to be in and what he will look like and what evidences he should have to prove his authentic sonship. An impostor in the meantime returns to claim the land and the inheritance and says he is the son and the rightful owner. He hoodwinks all the officials but one a trusted king's adviser who is on the trail to prove this man is a liar and not the original son.

So if the impostor who claims to be the son of the King has returned but he is not the son while the real son is still out of the country and out of the home. But when the real son returns the two fight to prove who is the real son. The two people who both purport to be the sons of the king. How do we know which is the son. Both have different colours. One black and the other white.

How do we know that the missing Israelites were black and not of Caucasian skin colour?

The truth has been hidden in the missing genealogy now uncovered in the Hidden-Truths Hebraic Scrolls 4th Edition.

> **Beresheeth (Gen) 10:22** The sons of Shem were; Elam (Iran), Asshur (Assyria), Arpakshad,[25] Lud (Turkey), and Aram (Syria) and Qeynan.

---

[25] Arpakshad is Aref+Chesed, these are twins or two persons. It appears this may have been mistaken for one person by the scribe hence the name is joined. We find one son under Nachor appearing as Chesed which is this derivative in Gen 22:22. According to the scholar John Lamb this should have been written the twins sons of Shem... According to John Lamb, The Dalet in chesed is like lips spelt Kaf,

Do you see it? Qeynan who was a black kid was the son of Shem and Shem was a man of colour that is black skin colour.

> **Ezek 37:1-2** The hand of YHWH was upon me, and carried me out in the Ruach (Spirit) of YHWH, and set me down in the midst of the valley which was full of bones, **2** And caused me to pass by them roundabout: and, behold, there were very many in the open valley; and, lo, they were very dry.

The dry bones is our evidence that dead Israelites don't walk unless YHWH raised them up from the dead. They had been dead a long time hence why they are so dry. The term dry also means they died in wickedness or anti-Torah. This is the ten tribes of Ysrael by the way.

The Hebraic Idiom dry means to be without Torah and the idiom Green means to be with Torah.

> **Tehillim (Ps) 105:41** He opened the rock, and the waters gushed out; they ran in the dry places like a river.

The water is the idiomatic expression for living waters and the Torah and the dry places an expression for without Torah and now with the living waters nourishing it they become places of Torah.

> **Yeshayahu 56:3** Neither let the son of the foreigner that has joined himself to YHWH, speak, saying, YHWH has utterly separated me from his people: neither let the eunuch say, Behold, I am a dry etz (tree).

The eunuch is saying that he is not fruitful which is the expression for Torah.

> **Luke 23:31** For if these things be done to the green

---

transgression and dalet and shem like moon signifies these studied astronomy who were later called Chasdees. He gives Aref the meaning "man of a bird's mouth" in his studies on ancient Hebrew Hieroglyphs page 69 Hebrew characters derived from Hieroglyphs.

etz (tree), what shall be done in the dry?[26]

This is the prophecy of the Torah Right-Ruling Messiah who was killed and then raised. Luke a Levite rightly questions if they do these things to the green (Torah right-ruling man) then what about the wicked (dry).

> **Ezek 37:3** And he said to me, Son of man, can these bones live? And I answered, O Master YHWH, you know.

YHWH asks Ezekiel what he thinks of the dead people. The bones here is an idiomatic expression for people which are really dead and Ezekiel not wanting to offend YHWH replies 'You know,' which was the correct response from a priest of the Most High.

> **Ezek 37:4** Again he said to me, Prophesy upon these bones, and say to them, O you dry bones, hear the word of YHWH.

This indicates to us that the dead Israelites are going to hear the Torah of YHWH as in YHWH's voice. When it says Shamo Davar YHWH.

> **Ezek 37:5** Thus says Master YHWH to these bones; Behold, I will cause breath to enter into you, and you shall have life:

Tell me what just happened? I guarantee you did not see nor understood what YHWH did there.

He spoke the letters of the Torah to them and they arose from their graves. This is not allegory. He raised them by the power of his set-apart word which is Torah and life. So through the Torah he gave them (dead Ysraelites) life even though they had died in wickedness or anti-Torah. So next time someone tells you that the Torah is no good or of no value remind them each character in the Torah is very valuable. These are the same letters that were used to

---

[26] The 'green' tree is a prophecy of the Messiah (Jer 11:16, Ps 52:8) while the 'dry' tree is used of a man who is childless and for other people. This is correct rendering of the Hebrew idiom, "If these things be done to the Green Tree."

create the world.

> **Ezek 37:6** And I will lay sinews upon you, and will bring up flesh upon you, and cover you with skin, and put breath in you, and you shall have life; and you shall know that I am YHWH.

Clearly these people who were biological Israelites died in the exile and may have even adopted other false religions such as, Buddhism, Islam, Hinduism or whatever. YHWH will still resurrect them, puts a new spirit into them and then they know who YHWH really is because they did not know previously and died without the knowledge of YHWH. They had allowed their spirit beings to be defiled by false religions. Many of these had been born in exiled lands and died without any message of the gospel (Besorah) or Torah in their lives. When these people had died they went to She'ol a place which has both the Paradise and sections of hell. She'ol has many floors and on each floor many sections.

There is a partition for the likes of the wicked non Ysraelites too which are handed to demons whose job is to torment them with punishement. While the wicked dead of Israel are kept in another section to be raised later.

The right-rulings one's in paradise have no need of anything and are in the state of shalom, they too will be raised from that state.

The right-ruling of Y'sra'el are all in that section called Paradise.

> **Ezek 37:7-8** So I prophesied as I was commanded: and as I prophesied, there was a noise, and behold a shaking, and the bones came together, bone to his bone. **8** And when I beheld, lo, the sinews and the flesh came up upon them, and the skin covered them above: but there was no breath in them.

This is where the ten tribes were resurrected in their individual countries of sojourn where they had died. So if you were in America and you died in exile you will be raised back in America.

Ezek 37:9 Then said he to me, Prophesy to the wind, prophesy, son of man, and say to the wind, Thus says Master YHWH; Come from the four winds, O breath, and breathe upon these slain, that they may live.

אמר אדני יהוה מארבע רוחות באי הרוח ופחי בהרוגים

Amar Adoni YHWH M'ar-bah Ruakhot Bo-ee Ha-Ruakh UFKHI B'haro-gim

Spoke Melek YHWH to the four winds to the breath and breath upon them who were slain.

When a baby is born who gives life? It is the mother who begets the baby and not the man but the man's will is there in order to get that far, in other words without his seed this would not be possible. This means a man has to have relations with a woman before a baby can be born but the procreation act of delivering the baby cannot be completed without the woman playing the most major role of housing the baby for nine months before delivery.

The same way the dead Israelites are raised by the feminine Spirits of YHWH and given life through them. These are the feminine Spirits that were watching all this time acting as agents of YHWH. They are part of YHWH. I call them the concubines of YHWH.

Zech 4:10 For who has despised the day of small things? For they shall rejoice, and shall see the plummet in the hand of Zerubbab'el with those seven; they are the <u>eyes</u> of YHWH, which run to and fro through the whole earth.[27]

Why the eyes and not the hands?

The Hebrew word is Alah Ayni YHWH. The key word for eyes in ther is Ai. This is mentioned of Abraham building an altar on between Bethel and Ai in Gen 12:8 which was the name of a city. This city was more than likely of sun worshippers. These feminine Spirits float in the air and send their report back to Abbah YHWH.

---

[27] See footnote Zec 3:9.

Then we are told the words Mashuttem B'Kul Ha'Eretz. "running to and fro that is east to west and north to south.- The Hebrew word shoot to go to and from in the ancient means, "the majesty flowing in the air".

אלה עיני יהוה המה משוטטים בכל־הארץ

The eyes are the 7 hidden Spirits of YHWH which are in the world. They will be used to raise the ten tribes. They are allegorical to the concubines or wives of YHWH. YHWH as a patriarch has 8 wives. One wife is the Ruach Ha Kadosh and the other seven are the lesser wives in picture speech.

In ancient cultures trying to decipher YHWH they actually did place YHWH with a consort however the problem is YHWH is Akhad. His wives are within him they are not seen as they are Spirits. Did you know in the Islamic religion Allah had one wife and two daughters which is confused with 3 daughters so if its 3 daughters then there is the wife in heaven too as daughters are begotten from a wife.

> **Ezek 37:10** So I prophesied as he commanded me, and the breath came into them, and they lived, and stood up upon their feet, an exceeding great army.

An army ready to march back to Y'sra'el.

> **Ezek 37:12** Therefore prophesy and say to them, Thus says the Master YHWH; Behold, O my people, I will open your graves, and cause you to come up out of your graves, and bring you into the land of Y'sra'el.

YHWH will literally open the graves of these people and make them march back to Ysrael. When he said 'Bring you into the land.' The inference is clear that they are outside the land and had died.

> **Ezek 37:13** and then you shall know that I am YHWH, when I have opened your graves, O my people, and brought you up out of your graves,

They died without knowing YHWH or having a relationship with him. So He will raise them and bring them back. There goes the false theory that no one comes out of hell and can get a second chance. The Israelites will be given a second chance because the Israelites are the chosen and have a Contract/Agreement with YHWH.

> **Ezek 37:14** And shall put my Ruach (Spirit) in you, and <u>you shall live</u>, and I shall place you **in your own land**: **then shall you know** that I YHWH have spoken it, and performed it, says YHWH.

They were not in their lands at death but outside it.

"They shall know" which is a clear implication that they died without knowledge of YHWH under some false religion which means when they are raised they will then realize that it is YHWH the only true Power to save them.

YHWH has spoken it meaning he will raise them and give them preference to enter the land.

Can we give anything else as proof that YHWH will raise them from She'ol or hell? Can we get a second witness Rebbe Shimoun? Yes sir we can.

> **Zech 9:11** As for you also, by the <u>blood of your Contract/Agreement</u> I have sent forth your prisoners out of the pit wherein is no mayim (water).

Whose blood? This is the blood shed by Yahushua.

We can see that blood of the Contract/Agreement delivers both houses those dead and those alive. Dead Israelites who were in sin were kept in a particular section of She'ol waiting resurrection.

> **Ezek 37:16-17** Moreover, you son of man, take yourself one etz (stick), and write upon it, For Yahudah, and for the children of Y'sra'el his companions: then take another etz (stick), and write upon it, For Yosef, the etz (tree) of Efrayim, and for all the house of Y'sra'el his companions: **17** And join them one to another into one etz (tree); and

they shall become Akhad (united) in your hand.

Notice Paulos also spoke about two trees in Romans 11:24

> **Romiyah 11:24** For if you were cut out of the olive etz (tree) which is wild by nature, and were grafted contrary to nature into a good olive etz (tree): how much more shall these, which be the natural branches, be grafted into their own olive etz (tree)?

What do we see here?

We see two trees? What is symbolic of the two trees? The two trees are revealing the Torah that is a scroll with a tree on each side.

Basically Ezekiel is shown a gentile tree (Efrayim) is grafted unto Yahudah the natural olive tree.

> **Ezek 37:21** And say to them, Thus says the Master YHWH; Behold, I will take the children of Y'sra'el from among the gentiles, where they be gone, and will gather them on from every side, and bring them into their own land:

Has this happened? No. Why not? Because this come about everyone will know YHWH as stated above which is not ye the case.

When you speak to someone and used the name YHWH they think you are speaking Arabic so the knowledge of the Most High is still lacking.

This is not yet fulfilled not even a bit of it.

> **Ezek 37:22** And I will make them one nation in the land upon the mountains of Y'sra'el; and one king shall be king to them all: and they shall be no more two nations, neither shall they be divided into two kingdoms any more at all:

Once this is done there will be a king over them and yet we have none of this in Israel.

Who will be this king?

It will be King Dawud.

> **Ezek 37:24** And Dawud my servant shall be king over them; and they all shall have one shepherd: they shall also walk in my right-rulings, and observe my statutes, and do them.

Get your popcorn and soda ready?

How many people in this passage?

Two, one is King David who is the king who has not yet been raised. He is black in colour and Negroid in features. Two the Shepherd mentioned is Yahushua. He will be the universal King while King Dawud would be the co-King. It will be a two fold relationship. Same as in Pharaoh and ruler.

> **Ezek 37:25** And they shall dwell in the land that I have given to Yaqub my servant, wherein your ahvot (fathers) have dwelt; and they shall dwell therein, even they, and their children, and their children's children forever: and my servant <u>Dawud shall be their prince</u> forever.

David shall be their prince a clear implication of a co-regent with Yahushua.

> **Ezek 37:26** Moreover I will make a Contract/Agreement of shalom (peace) with them; it shall be an everlasting Contract/Agreement with them: and **I will place them, and multiply them**, and will set **my sanctuary**[28] in the midst of them forevermore.

YHWH will multiply people in the millennium through the model of polygamy the ancient practice of Ysrael. It won't be a one child policy like in China.

---

[28] We know that this is the millennium because YHWH has established His 3rd hekel amongst these resurrected and blood washed people of Messiah.

We know that this is the millennium because YHWH has established His 3rd hekel amongst these resurrected and blood washed people of Messiah.

> **Ezek 37:27** My tabernacle also shall be with them: yes, I will be their Elohim, and they shall be my people

Why the Tabernacle will be there if Yahushua is building the Temple?

Both will be there. Why? This is because the Temple will take time to rebuild and the Tabernacle will fill in while the Temple is being built. When he will swear once again to us as His people and we will swear to being His chosen.

> **Ezek 37:28** And the nations shall know that I YHWH do set-apart Y'sra'el, when my sanctuary shall be in the midst of them forevermore.

This is the time the nations will know about YHWH while most do not know about him yet. Can anyone deny these prophesies have come to pass is only walking in ignorance and self delusion. All Ysraelites are yet to be resurrected and put back in the land at least those that are dead. When the Messiah returns there are those who will be alive will be taken there.

Questions raised genetic Y'sra'el versus non genetic Y'sra'el

If genetic/DNA/Blood Y'sra'el (the ten exiled tribes) regardless of what religion/belief they fell into, can they get a pass on life regardless?

Case study

Question 1- So if a genetic person say from the tribe of Dan was born a Muslim and was an Islamic radical who is cutting people's heads off and blaspheming YWHW all his life just because he is from the tribe of Y'sra'el is he safe in She'ol/hell and will he be literally taken back to the land from the grave in spirit/soul/body?

Let's address these points step by step as there are several questions here to deal with.

Answer: From point 1 above it is clear that the radical Muslim knew that some people believed in the God by the name of Yahuweh but that person although was ignorant of his roots being genetic Y'sra'el but still went on killing others of either Christian, Judaic or no faith. Would he be allowed immunity because he is a genetic Y'sra'elite?

This is where the Torah the law of God comes in and all judgment stands.

There are two issues. One could an ignorant Y'sra'elite ignore YHWH and ignore the Spirit of YHWH and still go on killing? First of all I have not found such a case. In the End of Days all such people through the Spirit of YHWH would know who they are. Let us assume they don't know then what.

All sinners of Y'sra'el will be gathered on the borders of Y'sra'el but then they would be a special judged upon these rebellious and they will not allowed to enter the land. These are what I class rules for the rebels and those of our people who committed heinous crimes of any sort that were forbidden in the Torah. They will be forbidden to enter the camp and enjoy any rewards of the right-rulers class of people.

> **Yeshayahu (Isa) 66:24** And they shall go forth, and look upon the carcasses of the men that have transgressed against me: for their worm shall not die, neither shall their fire be quenched; and they shall be an abhorring to all flesh.
>
> **Mark 9:48** Where their worm dies not, and the fire is not quenched. **49** For everything shall be destroyed with fire, and every sacrifice shall be seasoned with salt.

Yahushua quotes Isaiah 66:24 when the end judgment is done the souls of the wicked ones will be destroyed and there will be cessation of life. The Hebrew word in Isaiah 66:24 shows us these are dead corpses or bones of the dead, they have no life left so there is no concept here for these ones to be eternally tortured. The highest form of Torah capital punishment is cessation of life with no existence and no joy of any future. People are not made to look upon their relations suffering eternal torment. Elohim is not a sadist to do that to others. There is no need for Him as He directly states He does not want the death of the wicked in Ezekiel 18:23, while the evangelicals are obsessive about everlasting torture, which is reserved only for the rebellious malakhim and a few other select wicked individuals that will probably come to cessation but the torment of the devil will continue.

Question 2- What about the person who falls into being a Christian/Catholic or even a Mormon and is going thru life as he was brought up. Let's take the Mormon first living a clean moral productive life (and they are even though mislead a moral people) and he dies he and goes to She'ol/Hell with no chance at all and is doomed to eternity because he was not from a tribe where as the person of Dan above gets a pass on a godless life?

Answer: The second question about the Christian/Catholic/Mormon man who is going through a productive life or is a peaceful man. This is very simple, if the man is deceived and disobeys the Torah law there is a punishment involved.

The Christian would be judged for not keeping the Torah in fact the same for the Catholic and the Mormon, they do not get the one thousand years reign plus they lose their fist resurrection which are rewards for right-rulers to obey the Torah and believe what the Messiah has said and asked us to do. After this these class of three are raised in the last resurrection and then judged according to Melek Yahushua standard of Torah. They can still endure a punishment for Torah rebellion which is forty years outside the camp after which it is up to Melek Yahushua to decide their fate. In my opinion here is how I see it. Since all three believed in 'Jesus' because that is what they were taught so there is a level of mercy that will be given to them, they are not simply condemned without a fair trial.

Here the judgment of little children comes into play as follows;

> **Matthew 18:3** And said, Verily I say to you, Except you be converted, and become as little children, you shall not enter into the kingdom of shamayim. **4** Whosoever therefore shall humble himself as this little child, the same is greatest in the kingdom of shamayim.

What does converted as little children mean and to humble oneself?

It means to do the commandments without question! So the law of Torah states that if one does not do the commandment then the question is who is the guilty party, the one not doing it or the one not being taught to do it e.g. the so called bad teachers. So part of the guilt will fall on the Church teachers and they will be punished for this by forfeiting whatever reward they were meant to get will be removed from them.

Then we have the rule of law which comes into play mentioned in Deut 28:1 into broken into the three levels as follows:

> **Dabarim 28:1** And it shall come to pass, if You shall listen carefully to the voice of YHWH your Elohim, to Guard and to do all his commandments which I command you this day, that YHWH your

Elohim will elevate you high above all nations of the world:

Level 1:

This will be the state of many Christians who removed the Torah the law of God from their lives. They will remain in a state of disillusion in this life and will be persecuted constantly at different levels because of their disobedience. They will never become the heads but remain the tails in the nations. This is not grace but punishment. Grace means at the end of it all they are allowed into eternity through the blood of the Messiah but the blood of the Messiah does not remove one's disobedience. Many in Churches claim the blood but look at their behavior when it comes to the obedience to the Torah.

Level 2:

The clarification from Yahushua comes into play also.

> **Mattityahu 5:17-18** For verily I say to you, until shamayim and the earth pass away, one yud or nekuda shall in no wise pass from the Torah, until all of it has been correctly filled up. **19** Whoever therefore shall break one of the least of these commandments, and shall teach men to do so, he shall be called the least in the kingdom of shamayim but whoever shall do and teach them, the same shall be called Rebbe (Great) in the kingdom of shamayim.**20** For I say to you that except your right-ruling shall exceed the right-ruling of the experts in the Torah and Pharisees, you shall in no case enter into the kingdom of shamayim.

Level 3:

Slavery and humiliation

> **Rev 3:9** Behold, I will make them of the synagogue of Shaitan (Satan), which say they are Yahudim (Hebrew people), and are not, but do lie; behold, I will make them to come and to pay homage before your feet, and to know that I have loved you.

The third level applies to anyone in class one. So a person who will be punished according to class 1 can also be made a slave and pay homage to the Torah right-ruling believers because they counted the Torah nothing. Yahuhsua says "**to know that I loved you**" meaning those of the Torah abiding group.

Question 3- Now what about the Christian/Catholic who at least has an understanding of the Messiah and professes Jesus (though wrong name because taught perhaps from birth) is also doomed to She'ol/hell and eternity because he is not part of a tribe of Y'sra'el by no fault of his own?

Answer: They profess 'Jesus' so they have the wrong understanding of the name but assuming they also did not obey the Torah but perhaps if these were taught they may have obeyed it. However we do not know that but only Melek Yahushua knows it so depending on these things they have eternity and are not condemned. However the first resurrection is a reward and Yahushua will judge to determine if these would have obeyed the Torah knowing it ahead and he will decide whether these get raised in the first resurrection, second or subsequent resurrection. Professing the wrong name does not lose their eternity but they are still grafted in Y'sra'el as believers.

Question 4- If this is the case then why did Yahushua come for if it only matters that true genetic Y'sra'el gets in no matter how disobedience throughout their life (killing, stealing etc) they are in and regular Joe Blog's on the street accepts the Messiah and misses Torah and is doomed?

Answer: This is not a matter for us to decide but God, according to the Torah they will get punishment but the ultimate Torah punishment is death. Yahushua did indeed come for genetic Y'sra'el but there are others (pure gentiles) who will join him also and this is pretty clearly stated as follows.

> **Matt 5:24** But he answered and said, I have been sent to the prostituting sheep of the Beyth (house)

of Y'sra'el.[29]

Notice the text says prostituting sheep which is the more accurate translation then the King James Version which says lost. There is a great difference between the word 'lost' and 'prostituting'. It means they are more into idolatry then lost. Well if they are into idolatry then if Yahushua can still rescue them. This is the part of the Contract that was formed. Those that are rebellious in their midst will be dealt with as explained earlier so it's not a free for all such as murderer, etc et all. However I want to be very clear you need to remove religion to come to the right understanding. Thieves are not condemned into eternity while the judgment the Church proclaims is utterly stupid and idiotic. In the law of God they are judged for theft, that's it, the penalty depends on what kind of theft but its never eternal torture. Only the foolish in Churches can be made to believe this because let us assume you were hungry and you went and stole bread then would God torture you to eternal death? No, it would be foolish to even think that this would be the case, the issue would be dealt with which is why were you short of bread, where was the alleged tithing paying Church members and why did they not come to assist you.

If you stole food from a store unless you have a compulsory habit issue the issue at hand will be punished and the punished is not death but is dependent on several factors of the committed crime. We as Torah judges would sit and decide the lower Beyth Din (House of Judgment), we have the upper Beyth Din (the twenty three judges) to decide upon murder and so on.

Question 5- Let's take another case a raised Catholic who turned to be a born again Christian and now a Torah observant non Tribe guy is he doomed to She'ol/hell and no hope of being in the land because he was not genetic Y'sra'el, or lets say he just stopped in his life at being saved so is he doomed over the radical Islamic guy killing people?

Answer: No, absolutely not. This person is redeemed already so why would he be doomed?

---

[29] Yahushua came for the lost sheep of the Ten scattered tribes of Y'sra'el.

John 10:16 And other sheep I have, which are not of this fold: them also I must bring, and they shall hear my voice; and there shall be one fold, and one shepherd.

Who are the other sheep? He is referring not only to the two Houses of Y'sra'el but also to Gentiles who have joined. These are the other sheep that will also join us. Hence a gentile is fully grafted in and has no problem with losing his redemption even if he is not genetic he has become a Hebrew and an Y'sra'elite. The other issue of him stopped being saved, the questioner has not said how does one become being unsaved? Is it that he becomes a criminal then he is punished for the crimes but you cannot just stop being saved, perhaps by some silly Church law but not by law of God? If you were rescued then you remain rescued to the end. God will forgive all your faults that were done in ignorance and even deliberate faults are forgiven as long as you recognize and turn to God for help. God at no time just casts you out as a piece of trash as do many Churches if you reject their so called denominational doctrine which really has no standing in the Torah.

Question 6- This makes no sense then for the Messiah to come if the Joe Blog's guy on the street has no chance in the land and especially if non-torah where he seems doomed no matter what?

Answer: Not at all because Joe Blog's has all the chance to be rescued and enter the land if he has put His faith in the Messiah and has to the best of his ability obeyed the Torah. Even if he has been taught wrong in the Church and has put his faith in the Messiah he still has eternity with Yahushua and is not condemned.

Question 7 – Is there other evidence in the scriptures that ties with the Ezekiel 37 chapter to verify this such as second or third witnesses?

Answer: Indeed there is and I will quote and then explain some of them.

Hoshea 13:14 I will ransom them from the power of

> the grave;[30] I will redeem them from death: O death, I will be your plagues; O grave, I will be your destruction: repentance shall be hid from my eyes.[31]

Does one understand the power of the grave? Does it say I will ransom right-ruling people only? No, this ransom is for collective Y'sra'el. They were in disobedience at many times of their lives but it was YHWH's mercy that allowed them to be ransomed through Yahushua. All they needed to do those that were or are alive is to accept the provision of Yahushua putting their sins before the lamb of God. What about those that had died prior to Yahushua coming? The blood of Yahushua the King retrofits for Y'sra'el.

> **Hoshea 14:16** Shomeron (Samaria) shall become desolate; for she has rebelled against her Elohim: they shall fall by the sword: their infants shall be dashed in pieces, and **their women with child shall be ripped up**.

So what was the fault of the women and the little infant who has no understanding but he was going to be murdered by invading enemy? Do you even understand the gravity of the sin that Y'sra'el brought on it's self? And what when the women and innocent infant are killed then what they go to hell? No, the right-ruling judgment of Torah does not allow that. In fact sin brought the death but they are still going to be rescued for everlasting life because perhaps the men were guilty but the women and infants may have been completely innocent. And if the men and women were both guilty then still the infant cannot be judged to eternal death, they would be fully rescued.

> **Mishle (Pro) 21:15** It is joy to the just to do right-ruling: but **destruction shall be** to the workers of iniquity.

The men and women who consciously departed from the Torah would be judged and sent to She'ol later to be

---

[30] Through Yahushua He has redeemed them.
[31] The same verse Rebbe Sha'ul quotes in 1 Cor 15: 55.

destroyed but the infants would not be judged the same way.

> **Mishle (Pro) 21:18** The **wicked shall be a ransom** for the right-ruling, and **the transgressor for the upright**.

Do you see the wicked are a ransom for the right-rulers. This means the wicked are marked for destruction but the right-rulers will not be judged the same way but live.

> **Amos 9:7-8** Are you not as children of the Cush (Sudanese Empire) to me,[32] O children of Y'sra'el? Says YHWH. Have not I brought up Y'sra'el out of the land of Mitzrayim (Egypt)? And the Plushtim from Caphtor, and the Assyrians from Kir? **8** Behold, the eyes of the Master YHWH are upon the sinful kingdom, and I will destroy it from off the face of the earth; saving that I will not utterly destroy the house of Yaqub, says YHWH.

In the ancient maps that even Britain drew the entire continent of Africa was called Ethiopia that would include Y'sra'el too. The ancient continent was entirely filled with black people including Y'sra'elites hence why YHWH is calling his people like the Cushites, that means in looks too not just character. Even though YHWH promised the destruction of Y'sra'el he said he will not utterly destroy Jacob meaning the twelve tribes.

> **Amos 9:9** For, lo, I will command, and I will sift the **house of Y'sra'el among all nations**, like as corn is sifted in a sieve, yet shall not the **least grain fall upon the earth**.

So YHWH said I will look for all the Y'sra'elites in the End of Days and none would fall away. So who is right YHWH or us who want to put religion and its foolishness on the right rule of YHWH? In order for them to be all over the nations in the first place was because of the sins of our forefathers so he brings them back in to teach them right-

---

[32] Hebrews were/are Black African Negroes pure and simple. By denying that the Black majority today are Hebrews we call Elohim a liar. Many Blacks in Europe, America and Africa are of pure Y'sra'elite blood.

ruling and how to obey the Torah. This is connected with Isaiah 2:3.

> **Amos 9:10** All the transgressors of my people shall die by the sword, which say, The evil shall not overtake nor prevent us.

This judgment took place on all those who were scattered and were not mindful of their punishment, they died.

> **Amos 9:15** And I will plant them upon their land, and they shall no more be pulled up out of their land which I have given them, says YHWH your Elohim.

Do we seriously think that all this generation that will be planted back would be one hundred percent fully Torah keeping? No. If they were then what would be the need of Isaiah 2:3 to teach the Torah?

> **Ps 49:14-17** Like sheep they are laid in She'ol; death shall feed on them; and the upright shall have dominion over them in the morning; and their beauty shall consume in She'ol from their dwelling. **15** But Elohim will redeem my soul from the power of She'ol: for he shall receive me. Selah.[33] **16** Be you not afraid when one is made rich, when the glory of his house is **Increased**; **17** For when he dies he shall carry nothing away: his glory shall not descend after him.

Even though Y'sra'el was punished for sin it's only Y'sra'el that is being rescued from the grave. Punishment for Y'sra'el is once and not again and again. While the rich gentiles who had trusted in their wealth and did not really care about God will be punished and ultimately destroyed.

---

[33] Abbah YHWH has done that for all of Y'sra'el through His Son Yahushua.

Chapter 8
The Sabbath and its abrogation

Mark 1:21-22 And they went into Kfar'Nachum; and straightway on the Sabbath day he entered into the synagogue, and taught. **22** And they were astonished at his teaching: for he taught them as one who had authority, and not as the experts of the Torah.

Who took the Sabbath away?

We need to ask what is Yahushua doing in the synagogue when according to professor Arnold Fructenbaum's thesis he should be resting at home.

> **Acts 13:12-16** Then the Proconsul, when he saw what was done, believed, being astonished at the Torah of YHWH. **13** Now when Paulos and his company loosed from Paphos, they came to Perga in Pamphylia: and Yahukhannan (John) departing from them returned to Yerushalim. **14** But when they departed from Perga, they came to Antioch in Pisidia, and **went into the synagogue** on the Sabbath day, and sat down. **15** And after the reading of the Parsha (Torah portion) and the Haftarah (reading from the prophets) the rulers of the synagogue sent to them, saying, You men and brothers, if you have any word of exhortation for the people, say so. **16** Then Paulos (Sha'ul) stood up, and gestured with his hand said, Men of Y'sra'el, and you that fear Elohim, listen.

Hang on a minute even Paulos is entering the Sabbath day to "**TEACH**", what's going on first Yahushua and now Paulos.

Does that show that all the believers entered Synagogues to teach and reach people? They did not enter Churches because they were places of pagan worship. The word Church was used for a pagan temple.

[34]"The festival of Sunday, like all other festivals, was always only a human ordinance, and it was far from the intentions of the apostles to establish a Divine command in this respect, far from them, and from the early apostolic Church, to transfer the laws of the Sabbath to Sunday."--Augustus Neander "The History of the Christian Religion and Church," 1843, p. 186.

"The [Catholic] Church took the pagan buckler of faith against the heathen. She took the pagan Roman Pantheon, [the Roman] temple to all the gods, and made it sacred to all the martyrs; so it stands to this day. She took the pagan Sunday and made it the Christian Sunday . . . The Sun was a foremost god with heathendom. Balder the beautiful: the White God, the old Scandinavians called him. The sun has worshipers at this very hour in Persia and other lands . . . Hence the Church would seem to have said, 'Keep that old, pagan name. It shall remain consecrated, sanctified.' And thus the pagan Sunday, dedicated to Balder, became the Christian Sunday, sacred to Jesus. The sun is a fitting emblem of Jesus. The Fathers often compared Jesus to the sun; as they compared Mary to the moon."--William L. Gildea, "Paschale Gaudium," in "The Catholic World," 58, March, 1894.

"The Church made a sacred day of Sunday . . . largely because it was the weekly festival of the sun;--for it was a definite Christian policy to take over the pagan festivals endeared to the people by tradition, and to give them a Christian significance."-- Arthur Weigall, "The Paganism in Our Christianity," 1928, p. 145.

"Remains of the struggle [between the religion of Christianity and the religion of Mithraism] are found in two institutions adopted from its rival by Christianity in the fourth century, the two Mithraic sacred days: December 25, 'dies natalis solis' [birthday of the sun], as the birthday of Jesus,--and

---

[34] http://www.pathlights.com/theselastdays/tracts/tract_22a.htm

> Sunday, 'the venerable day of the Sun,' as Constantine called it in his edict of 321."--Walter Woodburn Hyde, "Paganism to Christianity in the Roman Empire," p. 60.
>
> **Acts 20:7** And on the first week at the conclusion of the Sabbath (mia ho sabbaton), when the disciples came together to break Lechem (bread), Paulos (Sha'ul) proclaimed to them. He was ready to depart the day after; and continued his speech until midnight.

The best scriptural support that the Church offers is the one in Acts 20:7 to say the day was on Sunday. Obviously they have no understanding of what happened at the end of the Sabbath which they call Sunday but it was a Saturday night part of the same day.

Now let me in on another little secret the Sabbath starts from Saturday sunrise but the Friday sunset to Saturday sunset Sabbath model is not Y'sra'el's original model but was enacted after the Greek invasion of Y'sra'el when Antiochus in 175 BCE forced our people to drop the sunrise Sabbath and enact the sunset to sunset day. By the time the Romans came and enacted the Julian Calendar many of our people were keeping the Friday sunset to sunset Saturday Calendar in 45 BCE.

In the year 359 CE Elder Hillel II's Calendar was introduced that calculated the dates via the moon cycles. This calendar was also used to determine the festivals. The Tanak does not use the term "new moon" Yerakh which in the Hebrew is word "Khadash". The Hebrew uses the term Khodesh several times referring always to a month. However the translators for want of a better word translate this as new moon when it should be new month.

Think about it for a second, how would our people be looking for Aviv barley when in the month of Aviv we were meant to be keeping the Passover (Deut 16:1)? Our people were roaming in the desert for forty years from the first exodus so to fool people today most think they need to go checkout the Aviv barley when that was not a factor for determining the Passover as it was on a fixed date and our people had little clay tablets to tell time by the sun. They could even tell you when the end of the year was.

This whole aligning the Calendar with the Greeks and later with Rome enraged some of our people the House of Tzadok so much that many of them separated and lived in their own communities in every town. These are the people erroneously called Essenes by Christians. They lived in almost every town and had large communities in Syria Mark(Damascus) and Judea.

> **Mark 14:12-14** And before the day of Khag Ha Matzoth (Unleavened Bread), when they killed the Passover, his disciples said to him, Where shall we go for you that we may prepare a place that you may eat the Passover? **13** And he sent forth two of his disciples, and said to them, Go into the city, and there shall meet you a man bearing a pitcher of mayim: follow him. **14** And wheresoever he shall go in, say to the owner of the Beyth (house), The Rebbe said, Where is the guest room, **where I shall eat the Passover with my disciples**? **15** And he will show you a large upper room furnished and prepared: there make ready for us.

The man that the disciples of the Master Yahushua were to go to was a Lewite, from the House of Tzadok (Essene), he was the one to instruct about the room for the Passover. This again illustrates Yahushua had close links with the House of Tzadok (Lewites) and they only kept the Enochian (Chanok) calendar. These Lewites carried their water everywhere and were very meticulous with ritual purity and were well known for it in the area.

> Hephaistio of Thebes was an astrologer in the 5th Century CE, who compiled the historical Hellenistic Astrology Records in his research work called "Apotelesmatics." Hephaistio quotes King Antiochus saying that the New Moon is the time when the "Moon is Born" and is the "Birthday of the Month:"
>
> But Antiochus of Athens says also that this method has a certain truth to it. "Observe," he says "On a given day that the Moon is Born" and to this

number add 180 and always deduct 29 from the Birthday [γενέθλιον] of the Month.

(Apotelesmatics, Hephaistio of Thebes, Book I, Vol VI, Compendium, tr. Robert H. Schmidt & Robert Hand 1994 p.82 lines 21-24)

Our people were forced to celebrate the new moon birthday but that is a Greek custom.

The Essenes did not use the Roman or Greek calendars and outright rejected them and they even had issues with the Temple priesthood since they saw the High Priest as corrupt and sold to the Roman authorities.

Now the true day of Sabbath did not fall on a Saturday according to the Enoch's (Chanok's) Calendar but it would fall on a Saturday on one year cycle only and then the days would shift to accommodate the faulty GrecoRoman Calendars. The Enoch Calendar was a fixed calendar with fixed feast dates and fixed Sabbaths every year. The 7th day Shabbat would always be 7th but the Roman day would change so one year you could be all year on a Saturday Sabbath, and then the next you will be on a Sunday followed by a Monday and so on.

The month is made up of 30 days, there are four seasons in the year and each change occurs every 90 days. So according to Enoch making add one day after 90 days making it 91 days. So the calculation is 90 times 4 equals 360 so by adding 1 day at each 90 day cycle you arrive at 364 days.

The sun would remain in the latitude as the thirtieth day.

Using Chanok's calendar the true day for equal night and equal day occurs only in Jerusalem on March 16 after which we have the new year day 1. Therefore our count to Sabbath will begin March 17 in each Roman year, which the Sabbath will be a shifting day each year. So technically the last day of the year should be a Sabbath followed by the first day count to 7 to the next Sabbath. Now this year in 2013 the Sabbath is on a Saturday cycle each year. When the present Enoch year ends at March 16, 2014 it will be the date of Saturday 15 March. Now the date

Saturday 15 March the Roman date is not seen every year. So the new year starts March 17, 2014 which is a Roman Monday as day 1, therefore Day 7 for Enoch calendar in the year 2014 would be on a Sunday each week. The following year in 2015 this day would shift to a Monday and then the Sabbath would be a Monday each week.

This shows while in exile we are also under punishment that we cannot truly keep our Sabbath as we are meant to so in order to turn back to the Torah we have to do the best we can and keep and observe as many weekly Sabbaths as we are humanly able to in order to show the God of Y'sra'el we are serious about his Torah.

The disciples celebrated the weekly conclusion of the Sabbath with Havdalah prayers. This is wrongly understood by many Christians to be Sunday but it is actually the 7th day evening and could potentially be any day of the week as shown you earlier. Many bible translations insert the word 'day,' which does not exist in the Greek text and is referring to a special week count suggesting an omer count week to count the weeks left in the feast of Pentecost.

The Havdalah service marks the end of Shabbat or when three stars can be seen in the sky (normally about 45 minutes after sundown).

Items needed: a glass of wine or other liquid, some fragrant spices, and a special Havdalah candle.

Wine

The first of the four Havdalah benedictions is made over wine. Recite this benediction:

Barukh atah YHWH Elohaynu melekh ha-olam, borei p'riy ha-gafen. (Amein)

Benevolent are You, YHWH, our Elohim, King of the Universe, who creates the fruit of the vine. (Amein).
Spices

The second benediction is recited over fragrant spices. The spices represent a compensation for the loss of the special sabbath spirit. The spices commonly used are cloves, cinnamon or bay leaves. The spices are kept in a special decorated box called a b'samim box.

Barukh atah YHWH Elohaynu melekh ha-olam, borei minei b'samim. (Amein)

Benevolent are You, YHWH, our Elohim, King of the Universe, who creates varieties of spices. (Amein)

Fire

The third benediction is recited over the special, multi-wicked Havdalah candle (see on-line store for candles). If you cannot obtain a Havdalah candle, you can hold two candles close together, so their flames overlap. Party candles can be warmed up and twisted together to be used.

Lighting a flame is a remainder of marking the distinction between the sabbath and the weekday, because we cannot kindle a flame on the Sabbath as it is forbidden. However please note the disciples the true Y'sra'elites did not light candles but used oil to light lamps. So if you have a oil lit lamp or a menorah you would do well to do just that as these days some candles are made from pig fat and are not kosher so be careful.

After the benediction is recited, hold hands up to the flame with curved fingers, so you can see the shadow of your fingers on the palms.

Barukh atah YHWH Elohaynu melekh ha-olam, borei m'orei ha-eish. (Amein)
Benevolent are You, YHWH, our Elohim, King of the Universe, who creates the light of the fire. (Amein)

Havdalah ceremony

The final benediction is the Havdalah prayer itself, the prayer over the separation of different things. The prayer is recited over the wine. After the prayer is complete, the wine is drunk. A few drops of wine are used to extinguish the flame from the candle or the oil lamp.

Barukh atah YHWH Elohaynu melekh ha-olam, ha-mavdil bayn kodesh l'khol,

Benevolent are You, YHWH, our Elohim, King of the Universe, who distinguishes between the sacred and the secular,

bayn or l'khoshekh, bayn Ys'ra'el la-amim, bayn yom ha-sh'vi'i l'shayshet y'may ha-ma'aseh

between light and dark, between Y'sra'el and the nations, between the seventh day and the six days of labor

Barukh atah YHWH, ha-mavdil bayn kodesh l'khol. (Amein)
Benevolent are You, YHWH, who distinguishes between the sacred and the secular. (Amein)

The other scripture that Christians are so fond of to do away with the Sabbath with once again incorrect translation is from the letter of Paulos the letter to the Colossians.

> **Col 2:16-17** (KJV) Let no man therefore judge you in meat, or in drink, or in respect of an holyday, or of the new moon, or of the sabbath *days*: 17 Which are a shadow of things to come; but the body *is* of Christ. **16** Let no man therefore judge ye in meat, or in drink, or in respect of a set-apart day, or of the Rosh Kodesh (new moon), or of the Sabbath days: **17** Which are a shadow of things to come; but the body of Messiah.[35]

The term 'man' is a rabbinic term only applied to the ten northern tribes whom were called gentiles.

---

[35] The word "is" was inserted later which confused the text. The passage is simply saying do not let the heathens judge you but only the **body of Messiah, which was Sabbath keeping from sunrise**. The feasts are still a shadow in the present form to make us remember the Messiah and are everlasting. To encourage you we had Sabbath keepers before the time of Moses in Africa and up to 1000 years after the death and resurrection of the Messiah. Polycarp the direct disciple of John was a Sabbath keeper and kept all the seven annual feasts and kosher laws out of Lev 11.

I am not going to correct Paulos as he taught quite a few anti-Torah doctrines the reason why most Christians are 180 degrees way off on the message.

The term "man" is referring to any heathen or man outside our community of trustworthy Y'sra'elites is not to judge us on what we eat, drink or not. What days we keep and why we keep is our eternal contract with YHWH and outsiders will surely object to our days, our meats and our way of life, that is not to be a concern to us for we are to remain trustworthy.

Conclusion

In conclusion I have only scratched the surface of what was hidden, the laws of God which were deliberately suppressed by unruly men and women who hid them in their foolishness. How the 7th day Sabbath was removed in favour of Sunday but that does not do away with the 7th day Sabbath which was celebrated by many as the original Enochian calendar while others had gone to the Friday sunset to Saturday sunset calendar during the fourth century CE which was the Greek day of reckoning.

The question most of you will be asking what do I do now. The answer is simpler than you think. The first and foremost repent and turn back to the Torah. Apologize for your ignorance to Melek Yahushua and turn away from sinfulness which is living in anti-Torah. Keep the 7th day Sabbath as the first necessary element to restoring yourself. The 7th day Sabbath is this year Saturday sunrise to Saturday sunset. Roughly 6am Saturday daytime to 6pm Saturday depending on what time your sunrises and sunsets based on Chanok's calendar.

The Sabbath is the first seal of our faith. The second seal is circumcision. If you are a male over eight days old then you must be circumcised! After this you start to learn the laws step by step. If I can be of any help then you can write to me at africanysrael@yahoo.com and I will assist you further with any questions. Do you know another teacher who offers you his time free? You can also come and join our paltalk room by downloading a free paltalk messenger from www.paltalk.com and add my id simalt to it and then come join our room which we open each Saturday for Service from 3pm UK time and 9am central time USA. If you phone me and leave a message then I will ring you wherever you are in the world, just leave me a detailed message with your contact numbers. You can contact me on my UK landline number +44 (0) 1296 48 27 95. I don't do this for money but for your sakes that I see you in the Kingdom of Melek Yahushua. If you are in the US you can contact Rebbe Kefa on 1-210 827 3907 in Texas.

Also the real Jerusalem is found and the real Tabernacle of Melek Dawud (King David) please see the link on face book look for Rabbi Howshua Amariel with the only House of YHWH where his Ark was rested. Yes the true city of David is also in Tel Arad and not in the modern Jerusalem. the correct Jerusalem of the Jebusites which King David captures is in Tel Arad. Everything you see in the present Temple Mount is fake and second hand. The real deal is elsewhere changed by Rome.

Tel Arad the place of the Qadosh Ark.

Go to face book to see more pictures. We the true Y'sra'elites must go up to pay homage to that place where YHWH's name is and ask for forgiveness for our sins.

> **Hoshea 5:15** I will go and return to my place, **till they acknowledge their offence**, and seek my face: in their affliction they will seek me early.

Rabbi Simon representing the House of Lewi of Aaron, the House of Yahudah from America and possibly some brothers from the House of Ephrayim from the nations will be going up to Y'sra'el in 2014 May to pay homage to YHWH and to fulfill the prophecy related to the House representatives to ask for forgiveness of sins and transgressions committed by our forefathers and us so that YHWH may return there and restore our people back.

Jer 26:18 Mikahyah (Micah) the Moresheth prophesied in the days of Yakhizqiyahu (Hezekiah) Sovereign of Yahudah, and spoke to all the people of Yahudah, saying, Thus says YHWH of Armies; **Tsiyon shall be plowed like a field**, and **Yerushalim shall become heaps**, and the **mountain of the house as the high places of a forest**.

Tel Arad ploughed fields where the Real Tsiyon is and the House of YHWH.

And you thought you knew much but the reality is you got to start fresh and the God of Y'sra'el will help you.

In the end I say Shalom, Shalom and be well.

May the Master Melek Yahushua increase you in his ways.

Rabbi Simon Altaf

Annual Feasts Calendar
The Annual Khanokian (Enochian) Calendar

> Yahubelim (Jubilees) 4:17 And he was the first among men [Khanok] that are born on earth who learnt writing and knowledge and wisdom and who wrote down the signs of heaven according to the order of their months in a book that men might know the seasons of the years according to the order of their separate months.

Annual New Year Begins... March 21 every year without change.[36]

New year and Months	Recurring Yearly without any moon sightings
First Month	21 March - Beginning of New Year
Second Month	20, April
Third Month	20, May
Fourth Month	20, June
Fifth Month	20, July
Six Month	19, August
Seventh Month	19, September
Eight Month	20, October
Ninth Month	19, November
Tenth Month	20, December
Eleventh Month	19, January
Twelfth Month	18, February

No addition of an extra month every three years.

---

[36] This calendar was written with the help of Rebbe Moshe Koniuchowsky.

All the seasonal markers must be taken from Jerusalem and not from the country of your abode.

The above celebrations repeat annually.

Yahubelim (Jubilees) 6:32-35 And command you the Bani Y'sra'el that they observe the years according to this reckoning- three hundred and sixty-four days, and (these) will constitute a complete year, and they will not disturb its time from its days and from its celebrations; for everything will fall out in them according to **33** their testimony, and they will not leave out any Yom nor disturb any celebrations. But if they do neglect and do not observe them according to His commandment, then they will disturb all their seasons and the years will be dislodged from this (order), [and they will disturb the seasons and the years **34** will be dislodged] and they will neglect their ordinances. And **all the Bani Y'sra'el will forget and will not find the path of the years, and will forget the new moons, and seasons, and Sabbaths. 35** and they will go wrong as to all the order of the years. For I know and from henceforth will I declare it on to you, and it is not of my own devising; for the book (lies) written before me, and on **the heavenly tablets the division of days is ordained, lest they forget the celebrations of the contract.**[37]

If we think about it then it makes perfect sense because we were following the rabbinic Calendar we all forgot the real deal and lost our ways of the years until now we have the chance to be restored with the original Patriarchal calendar.

Celebrations of YHWH	Yearly
Month 1, Abib 14	Pesakh - Seder Same evening

---

[37] So this prophecy of misalignment of years has come to pass in our time.

Month 1, Abib 15 last day Abib 21 (April 4 to April 10)	Unleavened Bread
Month 1, (around Abib 25) Day after the first weekly Sabbath following Unleavened Bread festival and always on a Sunday	Bikkurim - First-Fruits
Month 3 - Count 7 weekly Sabbaths after First-Fruits and it will always be the Sunday following the 7 Sabbaths.	Shavuot Pentecost (50-Days count)
Month 7 (Tishri 1) Sept 19	Terua (Blowing of Shofarim)
Month 7 (Tishri 9 Evening to Tishri 10 Evening) September 28	Yom Kippurim (Day of Atonements) fast starts one hour before sun sets.
Month 7 (Tishri 15-22) This follows to Simchat Torah day of celebration. (Oct 3 to Oct 10)	Sukkot (Celebrations of Tents) and Simchat Torah which is Oct 10.
Note - The Master Yahushua was born on Tishri 15, which is on the first day of Khag Sukkot (The Holiday of the Tent of Meetings).	
Celebration of Khanukah yearly, (9th Month day 25) annually. (Month of Kislev), expulsion of the Greeks and rededication of the Temple. (Dec 13-Dec 20)	
Celebration of Purim (Lots) yearly occurring on the twelfth Hebrew month days 14 and 15. (Month of Adar), Rescue of the Hebrew people in Iran to India and the death of Haman and his ten sons who plotted to kill all the Hebrew people. You can read this story in Esther. (March 3 to March 4 Annually)	

Glossary

Haftarah – Torah portions and the books of the prophets read each Sabbath day.

Tanak – The books of the Hebrew Bible erroneously called the Old Testament. One should never call these Old Testament as its calling the Creator's manual of no value which will render you a sinner.

Rebbe – One who had great understanding in the ways, the laws of YHWH and who is able to explain the Tanak.

Pharisee – (Prushim) These were men who were held in different positions in the Temple, there were also there to expound on the Torah the Tanak and other day to day matters. The word prush means to separate.

In the first century there were many Pharisees that belonged to two main schools such as Shammai and Hillel. A third group of Pharisees had much earlier broken off the mainstream and gone to live in the desert in Qumran called the Hasid who later in 1947 onwards came to be known as the Essenes. These were essentially the Hasidic branch of Judaism that once again flourished in the 16th century in Europe but they were not practicing essenism. The fourth branch of the Pharisees called themselves the Netzarim who were the followers of Yahushua and they worshiped in regular synagogues and the Temple. It was much later that they formed their own synagogues when they were thrown out of the mainstream synagogues. One of the leading Pharisees known as Paulos who was called Sha'ul and Paulos, he carried both names who actively promoted and created congregations in Asia Minor such as Turkey. Peter whose real name was Shimon Kefa went to Iraq and formed about twenty congregations there.

> **First Kefa 5:13** The chosen *Y'sra'elite* congregation that is in Babylon (Iraq), elected together with you, greets ye; and so does Musa-Markus (Mark Moses) my son.

Malakh (Angel)
Malakhim (plural for angels)

Mashiakh – One who is anointed to do a particular task set by the Father in heaven. This title is given to Kings, Prophets and Judges.

Halacha – How to do Torah deeds agreed by a council of teachers such as the seven annual feasts and the way they should be performed.

Netzar – Branches.

Parsha – Torah readings

For youtube teachings please go to
http://www.youtube.com/simalt

http://www.african-israel.com/Books/books.html

Get one of the best Hebrew Roots Bible; this will become your Bible of choice opening up many areas of the Scriptures which will give you a whole new understanding. The Hidden Truths Hebraic Scrolls Complete Bible can be ordered at the URL below. www.african-israel.com.

We suggest you visit our website to see the following Titles:
www.african-israel.com

Beyth Yahushua – the Son of Tzadok, the Son of Dawud
Would you like to know the identity of Yahushua's family the man you call Jesus? Did He have brothers and sisters, did He get married, and are not Rabbis meant to marry?

Is it true if Mary Magdalene was His wife and if not then what relationship did she have with him?

Are you fed-up of hearing objections from unbelievers such as "since you do not know who Matthew, Mark, Luke and John were then how can you claim to have the truth?" Now you will know the truth without asking your pastor.

Who was Nicodemus and what relationship did Yahushua, Jesus of Nazareth have with Nicodemus? Who was the wider family of Yahushua?

For far too long He has been portrayed as the wandering man with no belongings and no family and living outside his home with women offering him money and food. This picture is both misleading and deceptive.

Do you want to know the powerful family of Yahushua that was a threat to Rome?

Who were Mark, Luke, and Matthew? Was Luke a gentile or a Hebrew priest?

What about the genealogy of Luke and Matthew in which the two fathers of Yahushua mentioned are Heli or Jacob in Matthew chapter 1:16 and Luke chapter 3:23 respectively?

This book will give you new insights and the rich history of Yahushua. Next time you will be able to identify the ten tribes and the real Messiah Yahushua known as Jesus of Nazareth.

Islam, Peace or Beast
Have you ever wondered why radical Muslims are blowing up buildings, bombings planes and creating havoc? We illustrate in this book the reality of radical Islam and the end of days that are upon us. Why are our governments reluctant to tell us the truth we uncover many details.

World War III – Unmasking the End-Times Beast
Who is the Antichrist, what countries are aligned with him and many of your other questions answered. All revealed in this book. Which might be the ten nations of the Antichrist? What did the prophets say on these events?

World War III – Salvation of the Jews
- How will the salvation of the Jews come about, will they convert to Christianity or will Christianity be folded into Judaism?
- Will the 3rd Temple be built before the return of the Messiah? Analyzed and explained with the correct sound hermeneutics.
- Will we have a war with Iran and when? Considering the pundits have been wrong since the last 3 years and only Simon has been on track up to this time. What signs will absolutely indicate impending war with Iran calculated and revealed.
- When will the Messiah return, what signs should we be looking for, is it on a Jubilee year?
- Will the Messiah return on the feast of Trumpets fact or fiction?
- Will America win the war in Afghanistan? Yes and No answer with details.
- Who is the prince of Ezekiel and why is he making sin sacrifices. Can one call these educational? Read the correct answers...
- Should we support the Jewish Aliyah to Israel or is it forbidden to enter the land for permanent stay under a secular godless government?

Rabbi Simon is the only Rabbi to look at the thorny issues that no one has addressed to date while many people mostly run with popular churchy opinions coloured by bad theology by picking and choosing verses in isolation. Is modern Zionism biblical? Is Israel right to take over territories occupied by Palestinians today? Should people be selling up homes to go and live in Israel? All these thorny questions and even more answered in this book the sequel to the popular prophecy book World War III - Unmasking the End-Times Beast.

Yeshua or Isa – True path for salvation
Ever tried to witness to your Muslim friends and were mocked? Do you have Passion for the Muslims to be saved? Want to know how Jesus Christ is Yeshua and not Isa? This book helps you to build a solid bridge with the Muslims. It clarifies your theological doubts and helps to present Yeshua to the Muslims effectively.

Dear Muslim – Meet YHWH the God of Abraham
Truth explained best seller step by step detailing and unveiling Islam! This book is designed for that friend, son or daughter who is about to convert into Islam but needs to read this first. This is the one stop to saving their souls. Don't procrastinate, get it today so that they may see what is the truth before they cause themselves to be confounded and duped into something not true.

The Feasts of YHWH, the Elohim of Israel
Have you ever asked why the feasts were given to Israel? Their meaning and their purpose is all explained in this detailed book that delves into the signs of the Messiah and the fulfillment of the feasts and how the return of the Messiah is revealed in the feasts. Why we are to obey the feasts and if we do not then we could potentially lose our place in the kingdom entry!

Testament of Abraham
Now it's time to hear Abraham's story from his own mouth what happened, how did he become God's friend. What other missing information that we are not told about is made available. Without Abraham there will be no Judaism, no Islam and no Christianity. He is the pivotal

point upon which all three religious text claim right but who does Abraham really belong to?

What is Truth?
Have you wondered what truth is and how we measure it? How do we arrive at the conclusion that what you have is truth? How do you know that the religion you have been following for so many years is the original faith? Can we examine Atheism and say why it is or is not true. We examine these things.

Hidden Truths Hebraic Scrolls Study Bible 5th Edition (Vol1 and Vol2)
The HT Complete Bible more myths busted. Over 1300 pages packed absolutely full of information - no Hebrew roots Bible even comes close this is guaranteed!!! The politically incorrect guide to the God of Israel and the real chosen people of YHWH. Are you willing to listen to what YHWH has said about our world and how He is going to restore all things back including His people?
Many texts uncovered and explained in great details accurately and many corrections made to make this a real eye-opener text.

- ➔ Was Chava (Eve) the only woman in the garden? We reveal a deep held secret.
- ➔ Where did the demons come from?
- ➔ Ezekiel refers to some of Israel's evil deeds in Egypt explicitly uncovered which are glossed over in the King James Version.
- ➔ Who are the Real Hebrews of the Bible, which people does the land of Y'sra'el really belong to? Time to do away with the deception.
- ➔ Did Abraham keep the Sabbath? We show you where.
- ➔ But I thought Keturah was Hagar another error of Judaism corrected.
- ➔ But I thought Keturah was married to Abraham after Sarah's death, no not really. A very bad textual translation in Genesis 25:1.

- ➔ Who was Balaam, a profit for cash as are many pastors and Bishops today?
- ➔ Who were Abraham's ancestors, Africans or Europeans?
- ➔ Why did Isaac marry at forty years of age, what happened to his first wife? Rebecca was not his only wife an error of Christendom exposed?
- ➔ Where is Noah's ark likely to be? Not Ararat in Turkey or Iran another error.
- ➔ Who are the four wives of Abraham and who is the real firstborn? Not Ishmael and not even Isaac. Was Isaac his only son another error?
- ➔ All the modification of modern Judaism of the scribes has been undone to give you what was the real text including the original conversation of the Serpent with Chava (Gen 3) unedited plus Abraham's conversation unedited at last in Genesis 18.

The legendary Rabbi Simon Altaf guarantees that this will teach you to take the best out there and open their eyes in prophecy, historical argument and theology. He will personally mentor you through the texts of the Torah, the prophets, the disciples and apostles of Yahushua. Does any Bible seller offer this extent of training? We do. And Rabbi Simon is available at the end of an e-mail or just a telephone call away for questions that you have and if he is not there you just leave a message on the phone and his promise is to get back to you anywhere in the world. We do not charge for our calls or any teachings over the phone. It does not matter if you are in India, Australia, Russia or the US or Timbuktu we will ring you.

Sefer Yashar (The Book of Jasher)
The book of Yashar has been translated from the original sources and with added commentary, corrected names of Elohim with the sacred names and with other missing text from the Hebrew. This will add to the gaps in your knowledge from the book of Genesis such as the following:
- What did the wicked do before the flood?
- Who were Abraham's African ancestors?

- Did Abraham have two wives?
- What relationship did Abraham have with Eli'ezer?
- Did Isaac wait forty years to be married?
- Why did Sarah die so suddenly?
- Did Moses marry in Egypt?
- Moses, what colour? White or Black.
- Many other questions now answered.

Seferim Chanoch (The Books of Enoch)
The books of Enoch details the fall, the names of the angels, what happened in the beginning and what was the result of those fallen angels. Where are they now and what will happen to them. He also reveals the birth of Noach and some very important details around this about the African ancestry of the patriarchs. He reveals the Son of Elohim and reveals Yahushua upon a throne. And many other important details to complete your knowledge.

Yahushua – The Black Messiah
Have you been lied to about the true identity of Yahushua? Have you been shown pictures of the idolatrous Borgia Cesare and may have believed that this Caucasian hybrid was Yahushua the Melek? What ethnicity was Yahushua and what race of people did He belong to? Is it important that we know His ethnicity? What colour was Moses, King David and King Solomon? We examine and look at the massive fraud perpetrated upon the western nations by their leaders to hide the real identity of the true Hebrew Israelite people and race which are being restored in these Last Days. Yahushua said <u>everything</u> will be restored and that includes His and His people's ethnicity and colour. Would you like to know because it affects your eternity and His true message then get this book now.

Hebrew Wisdom – Kabbalah in the Brit ha Chadasha
The book's purpose is to illustrate basic principles of Kabbalah and to reveal some of the Kabbalah symbolisms used in the New Testament. We look at the Sefirots what they mean and how they apply to some of the teachings in the New Contract/Agreement. We also look at the first chapter in Genesis and examine some of the symbols there.

We examine the name of Elohim in Exodus 3:14 and see what it means. We examine some teachings of John to reveal how he used Kabbalah freely.

The Apocrypha (With Pirke Avot 'Ethics of The Fathers')

Read the fifteen books of the Apocrypha to get an understanding of the events both of the exile and of Israel's early history before Yahushua the Messiah was born. Read Ethics of the Fathers to understand rabbinic wisdom and some important elements of the story of Genesis. The tests, the trials and the miracles of the Temples. Without these books the story in the bible is incomplete and has gaps which these books will fill up and give you a more complete understanding.

African-Israel Siddur transliterated Hebrew with English (Daily life prayers)

Many times we wonder what prayers should we do when we go to bed, when we leave our home in the morning and how do we pray daily? What prayer should I do if I have a ritual bath? What prayer is for affixing a Mezuzah? Each year you wonder how to do the Passover Aggadah and what is the procedure. This book also covers women's niddah laws to give you understanding into women's ritual purity. Unlike other prayer books Rabbi Simon actually bothers to explain small details that are important and often ignored. This is one book you should not be without.

World War III, The Second Exodus, Y'sra'el's return journey home

How will the genetic Hebrews be taken back to the land? Are the present day Jews in Y'sra'el of ancient stock? Is there any prophecy of foreigners invading Y'sra'el and inhabiting the land? How will Elohim have war with Amalek and wipe them out and who is Amalek today? Why is the Church so confused about bible prophecy?

How will the end come and why is the world hiding the identity of the true Y'sra'elites? Will there be a rapture or marching back on foot? What happens if we die in our exile? And many more questions answered. The time has come to expose the errors of others.

Patriarchal Marriage, Y'sra'el's Right-Ruling Way of Life Methods and Practice

How did the Y'sra'elites live? What form of marriage did they practice and how did they practice it? This book is about to show you what was God's design from the beginning and how the Y'sra'elites lived within God's required parameters. Today these things appear mythological but here we show you the methods and ways of how this lifestyle was practiced and is being restored in these last days while the much touted monogamy is wrecking lives and destroying families and society around us. How many marriages are breaking down as a result of the wrong model and how many children are living fatherless lives while women live husbandless and unfulfilled lives. This book will show you why the Greek and Roman monogamy model with a husband and a wife and a bit on the side does not work. While God's model of plural marriage is an everlasting model that not only works but saves many children from losing their father's and women from losing good husbands.

The Scroll of Yahubel (Jubilees)

The information that is missing in the Torah has been put in here to aid us in understanding the book of Genesis more. There are gaps in Genesis with what happened with Noakh? What was going on in Moses's time. This scroll allows us to piece together that information that is so important for our understanding. True names edition with many corrections made.

Who am I?

A Children's book to help the black Hebrew children with identity and direction in life. Many Hebrew children while looking for identity easily stray and looking for love which they do not find in their homes due to broken homes venture out and join gangs, get involved in criminal activities to prove themselves ruining their lives. This book's purpose is to help these children find themselves to teach them who they are and to find sound direction in life. This will help change